D0103021

The Ultimate Handbook

101 SUCCESS SECRETS

FOR GIFTED KIDS

The Ultimate Handbook

101 SUCCESS SECRETS

FOR GIFTED KIDS

Christine Fonseca

PRUFROCK PRESS INC.
WACO, TEXAS

Library of Congress Cataloging-in-Publication Data

Fonseca, Christine, 1966-
  101 success secrets for gifted kids : the ultimate guide / by Christine Fonseca.
    p. cm.
  Includes bibliographical references.
  ISBN 978-1-59363-544-2 (pbk.)
  1. Gifted children--Juvenile literature I. Title. II. Title: One hundred one success secrets for gifted kids.
  III. Title: One hundred and one success secrets for gifted kids.
  HQ773.5.F66 2011
  155.45'5--dc22

                              2011004912

Copyright © 2011, Prufrock Press Inc.

Edited by Lacy Compton

Layout Design by Raquel Trevino

ISBN-13: 978-1-59363-544-2

Printed in the United States of America.

At the time of this book's publication, all facts and figures cited are the most current available. All telephone numbers, addresses, and website URLs are accurate and active. All publications, organizations, websites, and other resources exist as described in the book, and all have been verified. The author and Prufrock Press Inc. make no warranty or guarantee concerning the information and materials given out by organizations or content found at websites, and we are not responsible for any changes that occur after this book's publication. If you find an error, please contact Prufrock Press Inc.

Prufrock Press Inc.
P.O. Box 8813
Waco, TX 76714-8813
Phone: (800) 998-2208
Fax: (800) 240-0333
http://www.prufrock.com

DEDICATION

To my mom, whose constant love and
support taught me that everything
is possible.

CONTENTS

Writing a book is always a journey. With this book, I had a lot of people along for the ride. To start, my agent, Krista Goering, really ignited this idea on our first phone conversation. She asked about an advice book for kids. A few months later, this book was born. My amazing editor, Lacy Compton, stretched me to make this book so much more than the original idea. The team at Prufrock Press gave substance to my dreams and created something so much more than I could have wished for this book.

Also on this journey were my writing buds—Elana Johnson, Michelle McLean, Danyelle Leafty, Julie Butcher-Fedynich, and Ali Cross—giving me the support I needed to see this book through. They kept me going, helped me when I got stuck, and provided the air I needed when things got tough.

So many parents and gifted kids journeyed with me on this book. Antoinette Dunbar and Cherie Lewis helped shape many of the aspects of this book, including the idea of having the quotes from parents and kids. The entire GATE community of the Temecula Valley Unified School District, as well as literally hundreds of gifted and talented kids from 50 states and three countries and dozens of parents, provided the real-life stories and quotes that run throughout the book. I am sincerely humbled by each and every one of you. Your stories and advice are a source of inspiration that extends beyond the pages of this book.

Finally, my family and their daily sacrifices made the writing of this book possible. Dirck, I promise I'll be around a bit more to help with the daily grind—at least until the next book. Fabiana and Erika, thanks for reading and making sure Mom was really speaking to gifted kids. Thanks also for sacrificing the card games and everything else. I guess I owe you a lot of game time now, don't I? Remember how much I love and appreciate all three of you.

Why This Book

Being identified as gifted means a lot more than being smart. For most kids, it means being good in school, even though you get bored easily. It may also mean that you can figure things out really fast—maybe even faster than your parents or teachers. But, being bright also means feeling stressed out. A lot. Peers, the pressures of school, the expectations of parents, and the feeling that no one understands you are enough to make most kids wish that the label of giftedness never existed.

That's where this book comes in. *101 Success Secrets for Gifted Kids: The Ultimate Guide* is full of the tips kids need to understand and make the most out of the gifted label. Advice and ideas from hundreds of kids just like you fill the pages, giving you everything you need to be a success—in school, with friends, and at home.

101 Success Secrets for Gifted Kids begins with an overview of giftedness that covers what it means to have the gifted label, the characteristics of giftedness, and the emotional aspects of being an exceptional learner.

The next three sections discuss specific problems that arise in your unique world, separated into the areas where you spend most of your time—school, friends, and family.

How to Use This Book

This book was designed to be used as you need it. Read the section that relates to whatever it is you are going through at the time. Got a problem with school and homework? Turn to that section. Want to know how to deal with your parents or siblings? Check out what others did. Friendship dilemmas? No problem—

just refer to that section. The point is to use the book as you need it and use it often. What makes sense today may change as you get older.

101 Success Secrets for Gifted Kids was also designed with your parents in mind. Even though they probably understand what you're going through, parents sometimes forget what it is to be young. This book can help them remember all of the issues that creep up in your world. Don't be afraid to share parts of this book with them!

And finally, if you find the book helpful and want to offer your own advice to kids like you, please e-mail me at christine@christinefonseca.com. I'm always looking for great tips and more ways to help kids. Sharing your own experiences is a great way for you to give back to others. Your advice may even end up in the next edition of this book!

—Christine Fonseca

Growing up with a gifted label can be hard work. Typically blessed with highly intelligent and intuitive minds, gifted kids are confronted with intense emotions that change rapidly, leaving them feeling confused, frustrated, and alone. That's where this book comes in. Packed with advice and success secrets from other children, *101 Success Secrets for Gifted Kids* sheds light on the world of giftedness. By offering practical advice for kids from the ones they listen to the most—other kids—it is my hope that this book can be a resource for both children and parents as they navigate through the sometimes treacherous waters of giftedness.

Use this book to address various concerns as they come up. Or, read it first and then share it with your children. Either way, be sure to talk about the information and advice with your kids. Use the ideas as a springboard to open the lines of communication. If you find something particularly helpful, shoot me a note at christine@christinefonseca.com and let me know.

I wish you much success in being the coach your children need as they progress through their years and embrace everything it means to be gifted.

—Christine Fonseca

Part I

Understanding how to live life as a gifted person begins with understanding what it means to be gifted in the first place. The next three chapters will cover everything you need to know about being gifted, from the attributes of giftedness, to the problems that sometimes arise, to the crazy mixed-up feelings most gifted kids share.

To start the ball rolling, I've got a little quiz to test your knowledge of giftedness. Answer the five true/false questions before you read this section. Once you're done reading all three chapters, try the quiz again. Did anything change?

AND SO IT BEGINS

QUIZ: WHAT DO I KNOW ABOUT BEING GIFTED?

Directions: Circle your answer for each question.

1. Being gifted means I should always earn good grades.

   TRUE   FALSE

2. If I make a lot of mistakes on my work at school, it means I can't possibly be gifted.

   TRUE   FALSE

3. Being super sensitive to things is *not* part of being gifted.

   TRUE   FALSE

4. Learning is always easy for gifted people.

   TRUE   FALSE

5. Giftedness only has to do with learning, not with how I feel about things.

   TRUE   FALSE

Chapter 1

> *"Being gifted means I look at the world differently than some of my friends. It also means that some people are going to assume that I never have to work hard. The truth is I work really, really hard at things. And, I hate it when, after working so hard, I don't do well." —Olivia, age 11*

So, you took a special test at school, your parents and teachers filled out a few forms, and now everyone says you're *gifted*. What on Earth does that mean? Will you get extra work now? Are people going to expect great things from you all of the time? Will you get to go on special field trips? The questions are endless, and they come back to the same issue . . .

What is gifted, anyways?

The truth is that there is not one agreed-upon answer as to what it means to be gifted. Organizations like the National Association of Gifted Children (NAGC) have tried to shed light on this by coming up with definitions for giftedness. NAGC (2010) believed that a gifted person is someone who shows a high potential for learning or performance in one or more areas of expression. Yeah, I know. That doesn't really clear anything up, does it?

Researchers agree that there is a specific set of characteristics that define giftedness—things like being smart, having strong reasoning skills, and having a vivid imagination. A need for logic, perfectionism, and being highly sensitive to—well, everything are also aspects of giftedness (Silverman, 1989).

But, these characteristics still don't say what it *means* to be gifted or how giftedness impacts your world.

SUCCESS SECRET #1
Giftedness isn't something you choose. It's how you are hardwired.

Giftedness, like eye color or height, isn't something you can choose. It's how you're hardwired. Success at school—or in life—really has nothing to do with it.

Giftedness means that you are biologically wired to view the world in a certain way. That's what all of those characteristics listed above refer to—*how* you actually think about things. You can try to think in a different way, try not to be gifted. You can fail in school and try to blend in with your friends. Regardless, you will still be gifted. It isn't something you can change.

> *"Being in GATE doesn't mean you're different from everyone else; it just means you think in different ways."—Hiro, age 13*

SUCCESS SECRET #2
Not all gifted kids are high achievers.

One of the more common myths that kids, parents, and even teachers may believe is that being gifted means you are supposed to get high grades all of the time (Webb, Gore, Amend, & DeVries, 2007). Not true at all. In fact, a lot of gifted kids struggle in school. It doesn't mean they aren't gifted, though. Usually it just means they haven't figured out how to make school work for them—something we will talk about in the next section.

So, if you are struggling in a particular subject or even with school in general, don't assume that it means you aren't gifted. Everyone struggles from time to time.

> *"I hate being called on in class when I didn't raise my hand. I feel like teachers just assume that because I am in GATE I know all the answers to everything. Not true."* —Kaitlyn, age 11

SUCCESS SECRET #3 — Being gifted does not mean you are perfect at everything.

Yeah, I know. You think you *should* know everything if you're really gifted, right? But, notice that the definitions I gave you have nothing to do with what you know. Nothing. Giftedness has to do with how you approach things, how you learn, and your potential for learning. It has nothing to do with being perfect. In fact, the truth is, no one is perfect at everything. So, relax a little, and realize that the label doesn't mean you are expected to be perfect. We'll deal with what your teachers and parents expect in later sections of the book.

> *"Don't get all stressed over the title 'gifted.' I did and I thought that it meant I had to get all A's and had to be perfect. I was wrong."* —Katie, age 12

SUCCESS SECRET #4

Not all teachers understand giftedness.

Speaking of teachers, not all of them understand the different aspects of giftedness. Like many people, sometimes they think it means you will be a high achiever. If you're not, they may think you aren't really gifted. As you already know, this just isn't true. Giftedness is all about potential and attributes. If you find that your teacher struggles with understanding your particular brand of giftedness, hang in there and just keep doing your best. Try talking to the teacher or your parents. Sometimes you have to explain yourself to others in order to get your needs met.

TIPS FOR TALKING TO TEACHERS

1. Ask them when you can speak to them about school.
2. State your concerns clearly.
3. Avoid words that blame such as "*You* did this" or "*You* never do that."
4. Use "I" statements such as "*I* would like to know if I can have a different word list," or "Sometimes *I* do better with more challenging work."
5. Ask your parents to help you if you are afraid to approach your teacher.

SUCCESS SECRET #5

Not all kids understand giftedness.

Just as teachers sometimes struggle with giftedness, so do kids. This especially may mean your friends who are not identified as gifted. They may have a hard time understanding why you get stressed about your grades or why you seem so sensitive all of the time. They may even get jealous over your strong thinking skills. As a result, some friends may tease you.

Try not to get upset. Their reaction is no different than your confusion over why they *don't* worry more about grades or the big issues facing the world. You just view the world through a different lens, focusing on different kinds of things, than they do. This is why it will feel like some of your friends don't "get" you.

Bottom line: Don't try to force your friends to understand your point of view. The trick is learning how to get along despite these differences and understanding that multiple points of view are important.

> *"Just be yourself. If people get stressed over that, that is their deal. You worry about being true to who you are." —Jared, age 12*

SUCCESS SECRET #6

Use your gifts kindly.

Sometimes kids are embarrassed about being identified as gifted or worried that it makes them different in a bad way. Others are excited about the label—too excited. Kids will sometimes boast about being the smartest in the class or the *only* one who knows the rules to all of the games.

The truth is, everyone has something to learn—even gifted kids. More importantly, being gifted is not an excuse for being mean. No one's needs are more or less important than anyone else's. So, use your giftedness kindly—to help others and yourself. Being gifted is special and not something that should be used to hurt or demean anyone else.

> *"Don't brag and feel all smart, because really, you're no different than other gifted kids. And, there are a lot of gifted kids."*—Maya, age 12

SUCCESS SECRET #7

Embrace your giftedness.

Being identified as gifted is neither a good thing nor a bad thing. It simply is. The label doesn't define you—the characteristics you demonstrate every day do. The key is to embrace all of the aspects of your giftedness and learn how to manage those things that are sometimes hard. These things can include emotional intensity, peer problems, and expectations—yours and those from the people around you.

In the next couple of chapters, we'll explore the specific aspects of giftedness and some of the more common problems that happen as a result.

TIPS FOR REACHING YOUR POTENTIAL

1. Get to know everything about yourself—the good and the not-so-good.
2. Try something new such as reading something different or building something you didn't think you could complete.
3. Do something creative every day.
4. Learn something new every day.
5. Instead of saying, "That can't be done," figure out how it can be done.

SUCCESS SECRET #8

Remember to have fun.

Like it or not, being gifted is nothing you can change. It's something you must learn to embrace. And, it's one of the many things that make you . . . YOU. Learn about what giftedness means for you. Learn to live to your

"Remember, you're still a kid. Have fun!" —Kana, age 10

potential. But, remember that you are first and foremost a kid—be sure to have fun every day.

Parents Sound Off

Parents have their own ideas of giftedness. Reading their thoughts can help you figure out what you think.

» "Gifted is something I identify as exceptional—like an artist who has a natural ability to sketch."—Devi

» "Gifted means you learn in a different way from other students. It also means being bored in school, getting distracted due to being bored, and struggling socially."—Julie

» "Giftedness means nothing other than specialized instruction in the younger grades. At least, that is how it seems in most cases."—Linda

» "Giftedness means not just learning at a faster rate than other kids, but being intense on a very fundamental level."—Andie

Yes, parents are sometimes as confused as you are over what it all means. But, confused or not, they do understand that giftedness is more than getting good grades in school.

Overall, the definition of giftedness is elusive. There are myths that cloud people's thinking and misinformation that can work against you. Your job is to learn everything you can about the attributes of giftedness, and then figure out how to make things work for you. Learning how to get your needs met through the educational system, as well as the support you need from friends and family, is a life skill that will help you now and in the future.

What Do You Think?

Now it's your turn. Take a few moments and ask yourself these questions. See how you feel about the label and all that is good—and bad—about being gifted.

WHAT DOES BEING GIFTED MEAN TO YOU?

WHAT IS THE BEST PART ABOUT BEING GIFTED? THE WORST?

WHAT ADVICE WOULD YOU SHARE WITH THOSE YOUNGER THAN YOU ABOUT BEING GIFTED?

Chapter 2

> "I really dig being gifted. I mean, the work is more interesting in school, my friends and I all seem to get along, and things are just . . . good. But, I still have to remind myself to relax. That part will probably always be hard." —Nira, age 12

Now you know that being gifted isn't just about being smart. It's how you're hardwired. Your giftedness influences how you view and interact with the world. The success secrets in this chapter will highlight specific characteristics about giftedness and help you learn more about the way these attributes may impact you—in good ways and in not-so-good ways.

SUCCESS SECRET #9 Learn everything you can about your giftedness.

Most of the things that make you unique involve the way you think about the world. The ability to solve problems quickly and creatively, being a fast learner, and understanding difficult concepts are all things you do every day. Some of the other characteristics of how you think include being highly curious (which is why some gifted kids like to take things apart and figure out how they work), having a vivid imagination, and demonstrating an intense need to learn (even if you think school is boring).

"Being gifted doesn't really change who you are. It just changes what you know about who you are." —Becca, age 14

Giftedness doesn't end with how you think. It involves how you act and behave as well. Gifted kids thrive when things are logical and hate it when everything seems chaotic. They often understand the complex problems that exist in the world and hate it when adults underestimate them. And, gifted kids think that perfection is required—so much so that they often decide not to try something for fear of failing (Webb et al., 2007).

SUCCESS SECRET #10   Your brain can lie to you.

Guess what? All of those feelings about being perfect—sometimes they are wrong. Sometimes your brain can lie to you and make you believe something that just isn't true. It happens because gifted kids think quickly, linking together ideas fast—too fast. Sometimes two wrong ideas get linked and gifted kids begin to believe things that may not be true. For example, a gifted kid may link together the idea that gifted kids are good at everything they try and the idea that not being good at something means you are not gifted. When these are linked, the gifted student may feel too much pressure to be perfect, believing that anything less means the gifted label was a lie.

So, what's a gifted kid to do? Slow the process down and learn to discern what is correct and accurate versus what is not. Learning to tell the difference between when your brain is lying to you and when it is not is critically important to managing the natural intensities your giftedness can bring.

An easy strategy to use when discerning whether or not your brain is correct in its assumption is something I call PROOF. With this method, you are literally looking for proof that what you believe is true. For example, let's say your brain is saying, "I am horrible at math. I will never learn it. So I must NOT be smart." To use the PROOF method, you are going to look for proof that you are, in fact, horrible at math. You will also need to prove that being horrible at math means you are not smart. So, look at your grades over time, look at test scores, and talk with your teachers and parents. Odds are really good you are not horrible at math at all. It's more likely that you are just struggling with a particular concept. Even if you do discover that math is not your best subject, it doesn't mean you are not smart. If your other grades are good, or if you have a lot of talent in other areas, then that's your proof that being bad at math does *not* mean you are dumb. It just means you will have to work harder in math than in your other subjects.

TIPS FOR USING THE PROOF TECHNIQUE

1. What message is your brain telling you? Be specific.
2. How do you *know* it's the correct message? What proof can you find that it is true?
3. If you find that the message is true, what can you do about it?
4. If you find that the message is untrue, what is the correct message?
5. How can you train your brain to stop giving you false messages?

SUCCESS SECRET #11

Gifted and intense go hand in hand.

As we said before, giftedness involves your thoughts, actions, and feelings. It also involves the way in which these things interact with the world. For gifted kids, everything is more intense. This means that you think more deeply than other kids, you behave in a way that is more focused or intense, and you feel things at a deeper level. When you are happy, you are super happy. But, when you are sad,

"All that emotional drama you start going through in fourth and fifth grade—don't freak out about it. It's normal. And the sooner you learn to manage it, the easier everything gets." —Fiona, age 12

you are very sad. There is no middle ground—no halfway point with you (Sword, 2006a).

This is not a bad thing, although sometimes it may feel like you are on an emotional rollercoaster that never seems to end.

SUCCESS SECRET #12 — *Let go of expectations.*

The intensity you feel in all aspects of your life can seep into everything—school, your friends, and your home life—and it can leave you feeling things in extremes. This includes how you feel about the expectations you have for yourself.

> *"The only problem with the label of gifted is dealing with everyone's expectations—my teachers, my parents, other kids. And yes, even my own."—Mary, age 11*

Many times gifted kids have expectations for themselves that are high. They believe they need to constantly do well. This unrealistically high expectation makes things harder than they need to be.

Let's take school. For some gifted kids, school is a great place to be. They thrive on learning. School has become synonymous with achieving—something that comes naturally to many gifted kids.

This is not true for everyone. Driven by the need for intellectual stimulation, some of you may find the routine nature of school boring. In your boredom, you may make careless errors—something the perfectionist in you abhors. You may find yourself pulling away from school and learning. You may even find yourself developing physical symptoms like headaches and stomachaches every time you try to go to school. All of this is related to everything it means to be gifted and the expectations gifted kids sometimes have for themselves.

We'll explore more of this in detail in the next section, as well as some strategies to help change the negative things about school and learning. The bottom line for now is to learn to let go of those unrealistic expectations.

SUCCESS SECRET #13 **The only thing you can really control is you.**

Intensity can impact how you interact with your friends and family. Many of you may find it hard to find friends. Perhaps you can't relate to the more typical things kids your age enjoy. For some of you, the problem is really about not knowing how to connect with kids in general. Friendships are often a large source of frustration.

Most of you often don't understand why your friends get annoyed with you, or why the kids at school think you're bossy or mean. It can be really hard and make you feel very sad, but guess what?

You have no control over how the other kids act toward you. In fact, you really have no control over anyone else. The only thing you do have control over is you, your behavior, and your reactions. Although that may not seem like enough some days, it really is a very powerful thing. Remembering that you are the only thing you have control over can be hard. That's where my hula hoop trick comes in.

TIPS FOR THE HULA HOOP TRICK

1. Imagine there is a hula hoop on the ground.
2. Step into the middle of it.
3. Everything *outside* of the hula hoop you have no control over—this includes friends, family, school . . . everything except *you*.
4. Everything *inside* the hula hoop you have 100% control over—this includes you, your thoughts, and your feelings.
5. The next time something bothers you, remember this hula hoop and decide if the problem is something you have control over. If it is (like your feelings), remember that you—and only you—can change it.

Use this technique every time you find yourself trying to change how other people behave. It will help you remember that the only one you can really change is you.

SUCCESS SECRET #14

It's OK to feel anxious sometimes.

Emotions are a big deal for many of you. As I've said before, being intense is a normal part of being gifted. That means that feeling overwhelming emotions—both the happy and the sad kind—

"It's fine to feel stressed out at times—everyone does. Just remember that learning to relax makes things a lot easier."—Aidan, age 13

is normal. The problem isn't that you experience these intense emotions. The problem is in *understanding* them. Fortunately, one thing you are really good at is figuring things out. You just need to know what to look for.

We'll explore more about understanding emotions later in the book. For now, just know that the intense stress and anxiety you sometimes feel is normal and not something to freak out over.

SUCCESS SECRET #15 Remember to take care of yourself.

Being a gifted kid is both great and difficult. But, regardless of whether you're having an easy time with your giftedness or a hard time, there are a few things you can do to manage your life better. The biggest thing is taking good care of yourself. No one copes well when he is tired, hungry, or stressed. Remembering to make *you* a priority in your life is essential to being successful now and later on.

TIPS FOR TAKING CARE OF YOURSELF

1. **Get plenty of rest**. Most kids your age require at least 8 hours every night. Developing a bedtime routine can help if you have a hard time getting to sleep at night.
2. **Eat healthy foods**. Junk food may taste good, but it can really work against your brain functioning and overall health. Learn about good food choices and commit to eating healthy every day.

3. **Stay active**. Exercise is an essential part of taking care of yourself. Most schools don't have daily P.E., so it is really important to spend a part of every day being active. Dance, jumping rope, playing ball—all of these forms of exercise will improve your brain functioning, keep you healthy, and make it easier to get to sleep at night. Not only that, but exercise is one of the best ways to combat stress.

4. **Relax**. We live in a very busy world. Learning to relax a little every day can help rejuvenate our minds and our bodies. Try deep breathing, yoga, prayer, or just sitting in silence for a few minutes every day.

5. **Play**. Life isn't just about work, especially when you're a kid. It is easy to get too busy with school and your extra activities to remember to play. But, playing is just as important as everything else. So find a way to carve out a few minutes of playtime. You can play with a friend, a pet, or your parents. Just a few minutes a day is all you need to stay in balance.

SUCCESS SECRET #16

Believe in yourself.

All in all, being gifted is a really cool thing. However, the traits that make you gifted are the very things that can become a problem for you. The intensity of your thinking can enable you to figure out the really hard stuff—and make school feel boring at times. The strong opinions you hold can make you a leader in class—and cause you to appear bossy and like a know-it-all to your friends. The strong emotions you feel every day can give you a sense

> "Sometimes it is hard to believe I am smart, especially if I get something wrong on a test. That's when I have to try to remember that everyone gets things wrong sometimes."
> —Mia, age 9

of passion and empathy about your world—and turn you into the occasional emotional mess. The trick is learning to balance out the way you're hardwired, using the good aspects of giftedness to smooth out the areas in which you struggle.

We'll learn more about this in the rest of the book. For now, it's just important that you believe in yourself and all of the wonderful things about being gifted—the good, the bad, and the stressful.

Parents Sound Off

Parents have a lot to say about the good and bad aspects of giftedness. Many of them know all too well how hard their children have to work at developing friendships, dealing with emotions, and fighting boredom in school. Take a look at what these parents say about giftedness, and then talk with your parents and see how they feel.

» "I love that my kid thinks of herself as smart. But, she never gives herself any room for failure. Everything has to be perfect. My daughter places unrealistic expectations on herself."—Lynn

» "It was so hard watching our children not live up to their potential because they were bored and took their education for granted. I think a lot of gifted kids do that."—Rajas

» "I love that no matter what she does, I know she'll give it her all. (But) I worry that she doesn't give herself permission to fail."—Carol

» "Man, parenting our children is great—and miserable at the same time. It is so hard to know how to help our children control their emotions or give themselves a break periodically."—Andie

Overall, parents see the ways you struggle to manage your stress. They also see all of the great tasks you can accomplish with your incredible mind.

In the end, all of the attributes of giftedness—the way you think, feel, and behave—are the things that make you amazing. Those same attributes are also the things that make life hard at times. Your job is to figure out how to keep it all in balance.

What Do You Think?

It's time for you to take a moment and reflect on the ideas in this chapter and your own thoughts. Figure out what your best attributes are and which ones cause you the most grief. This is the first step toward understanding how to maintain a good balance.

WHAT ARE THE WAYS IN WHICH YOU DEMONSTRATE YOUR GIFTEDNESS? HOW DO YOU THINK, ACT, AND FEEL ABOUT THINGS?

WHAT ASPECTS OF *YOUR* GIFTEDNESS GIVE YOU THE MOST TROUBLE?

HOW CAN YOU STAY IN BALANCE?

Chapter 3

> "I stress if I don't get A's on everything, I get really emotional with my friends, and I struggle with some of my school stuff. But, it is who I am."—Song, age 9

Ah yes, emotions: those crazy mixed-up ways you feel about . . . well . . . everything. Intense feelings are a normal part of giftedness. Unfortunately, intense emotions seldom garner a lot of respect from your peers, family, or teachers. Many times you may be left to feel like you're a little crazy. The truth is that emotional intensity is just part of what it means to be gifted.

But, what is emotional intensity, exactly?

Super happy and super sad feelings are part of it. So is the rapid change between feeling happy and feeling sad. And, it is so much more: Emotional intensity can be expressed physically, through headaches, stomachaches, heart palpations, even the need to constantly be moving. It can also be expressed as fear, anxiety, guilt, and shame. Usually it refers to a combination of all of those things occurring together (Sword, 2006a).

Emotional intensity isn't a bad thing, despite how bad some of the descriptions may sound. Intensity is actually just the way you view the world—through bold feelings, as opposed to the more calm ways most of your friends may view things.

SUCCESS SECRET #17 Your crazy, intense emotions are normal... and good.

As I've already mentioned, emotional intensity is a normal and natural part of being gifted. That doesn't mean that the way you react to your emotions works to help you. In fact, I bet you often react in ways that work against you. Like yelling when you're frustrated, or crying when you get overwhelmed. Maybe you even get stuck sometimes, constantly thinking about things that bother you and feeling like you'll never be able to make yourself stop. These ways of reacting can bring out the worst parts of your normal emotional intensity and create an even bigger problem.

"Learn to embrace your emotions. Things got so much better when I started to embrace mine."—Madison, age 14

The first step in changing all of this is to recognize that feeling things intensely is *not* the problem. Not at all.

SUCCESS SECRET #18 You control your feelings, not the other way around.

Learning to manage your emotional intensity begins with learning that your emotions aren't something that just happen without your control. Oh, sure, everyone reacts to things without necessarily being aware of *why* they are reacting the way they are. That doesn't mean that

> *"I hate the out-of-control feeling I get when I have too much to do—tests, projects, friend drama."—Chandi, age 10*

there isn't a reason for the reaction. There is. You are not a victim of your emotions.

Remember the hula hoop from earlier? Everything outside of the hoop is out of your control, but everything inside is yours to manage. Well, your emotions definitely lie inside the hoop. So, the next time you become overwhelmed by your emotions or scream at your parents for little reason, take a moment to remember that you are in control of your emotions—not the other way around.

SUCCESS SECRET #19

Put your feelings into words.

Controlling your emotions begins with recognizing them in the first place. And the best way to recognize them is by developing an emotional vocabulary. This means not only coming up with specific words to label the various feelings you have, but developing a word or phrase between you, your parents, and perhaps your friends that enables you to communicate when you are overwhelmed. By picking an easy-to-remember word or phrase, you can alert your family and friends that you need help managing your emotions. You can warn them, without getting yourself too stressed, that you aren't able to control all of your emotions at the moment.

For example, let's pretend you have a big project due in school. You are not happy with it and decide to start the whole thing over. The stress from having to redo a project due tomorrow has overwhelmed you. As a result, you yell at your mom when she asks a simple question. Having an emotional vocabulary—a word to explain what you're feeling when you can't really explain it—enables you to tell your mom that you need her to not push you. It also enables her to tell you that you seem overwhelmed, just in case the emotions have started to take over without you realizing it.

The development of this vocabulary is a great tool to help you learn how to stay in charge of your emotions. Trust me, your friends and family will appreciate everything you can learn in this area, and so will you.

TIPS FOR DEVELOPING AN EMOTIONAL VOCABULARY

1. Pick a word that accurately describes what you're feeling, like "spinning," "bursting," "overwhelmed," or "done."
2. Make the word something simple and easy to remember.
3. Choose the word with your parents. Ask them to help alert you when you are having a hard time managing your emotions.
4. Define what the word means—how the feeling looks. This way everyone has a common language they can use to talk about particular emotions.
5. Define both a word to alert a problem and some general feeling words (e.g., happy, sad, frustrated, anxious). Practice talking about your emotions often.

SUCCESS SECRET #20   Be honest with yourself.

Emotions are often difficult to control because people are so good at lying to themselves about their emotions. Remember how I said that your brain can lie at times? Well, sometimes it lies about our feelings or the feelings of others.

It's really important to be honest with yourself about your feelings. Don't say things are "fine" if they aren't. Likewise, don't create a problem with your feelings just to have one. By truthfully looking at how you feel in various situations, you can more easily identify those moments when your emotions are slipping out of control.

Parents and friends can be great allies in helping you become honest about your emotions. Asking them to help you figure out what you're feeling, particularly in times of stress, can go a long way toward learning to identify your emotions for yourself—and more importantly, learning to manage them.

> *"I hate admitting my mistakes. Or, admitting when I'm stressed. But, it's the only way I can learn to control it."—Alejandro, age 11*

SUCCESS SECRET #21 Learn to calm down *before* you explode.

Sometimes, despite your best efforts at learning to control your emotions, you can't help it. Your words fail, and you feel yourself edging closer to the point of exploding. It is really important to know how to calm down before you actually explode.

Your brain is a funny thing. When you're too angry (or too sad or too frustrated), the part of your brain that makes rational decisions slows or stops. You literally can't think about calming down (at least not immediately). This is when you must learn to recognize when you're beginning to get angry and calm yourself long enough for your brain to think and relax.

The first step is recognizing how your mind and body tend to react to stress. (We will outline some ways of doing this later in the book.) But, preventing the explosion takes more than just knowing your stress response. It also takes knowing what to do once you are really upset or overwhelmed.

There are lots of tricks people use to calm themselves. Taking deep breaths, picturing something relaxing, taking a break—all of these things can help diffuse your frustration, anger, or pain and allow your brain time to think before you explode. And, that's the key: giving yourself the time your brain needs to think.

TIPS FOR LEARNING TO COOL OFF

1. Know what makes you upset.
2. Take a deep breath.
3. Count to 10.
4. Walk away from the situation if you can.
5. Find a safe person you can vent to when you are emotionally overwhelmed, like a parent or teacher.

SUCCESS SECRET #22

Always remember to breathe.

Did you know that many people hold their breath when they get emotionally overwhelmed? Did you know that holding your breath keeps your brain from being able to think properly at times? It's not surprising, then, that you may be making really bad decisions when you are overwhelmed.

Deep breathing can help. A lot.

The key to deep breathing, however, is taking enough slow, deep breaths to really calm everything down and reengage the decision-making parts of your brain. This can be challenging for some people. It's hard to know when you have taken enough breaths to reach a calm state, especially if you are really overwhelmed when you start.

That's where the Breathing Colors technique can really help. This strategy is a visual way to *see* your stress in your imagination and watch it float away.

TIPS FOR THE BREATHING COLORS TECHNIQUE

1. Take several deep breaths.
2. On the inhalation, picture your favorite color. I use blue or pink.
3. On the exhalation, imagine a muddy-looking color. This is the color of the stress in your body.
4. Continue slow, steady breathing until the color you inhale matches the color you exhale.
5. Make a mental note of how long it took—this will help you learn more about your own feelings and how you respond to things.

Try this technique every time you need to relax. I think you'll be surprised at how effective it can be.

SUCCESS SECRET #23 Don't let your stress define you.

Another common aspect of your intense emotions can be summarized in one word: stress. Stress is something everyone feels at some point or another. Simply defined, it is the physical and emotional way we respond to tension. It is neither a good thing nor a bad thing.

For many of you, it's something you deal with every day.

The pressures of school, friendships, family expectations, and the myriad activities you are involved in can all create more tension in your life. This tension can translate to stress.

Headaches, stomach-aches, nervousness, anxiety, a short temper—these are all common reactions to stress. Oftentimes the stress is overwhelming, making you feel out of control.

> *"It's hard to remember that my anxiety doesn't define me."*—Maggie, age 13

Here's the secret . . . stress is just your reaction to the things going on in your life. And, like everything else inside the hula hoop, it is something you can change.

I know, easier said than done. But, many of the things we've already talked about—taking good care of yourself, learning to relax, deep breathing—can reduce your stress.

The important thing to remember is that stress doesn't have to define you. If you don't like how you react to the things in your life, you can learn to change it.

SUCCESS SECRET #24 Let go of the little things that annoy you.

Letting go of stress often means letting go of the things that annoy you. Have you ever noticed that most of the things you are annoyed about are little? They are things like the way your sibling acts toward you, what a teacher said about your paper, or maybe even something a friend said at lunch.

At the time, these things seem very important. They have the power to put you in a good mood or stress you out enough that your mood is horrible. After a little while, you begin to realize that you are stressing out over something that you have no control over, something you can't really do anything about.

It is at this point you need to learn to let it go and focus on the things you *can do* like changing your reaction. Sure, you may always instinctively get

> *"Don't beat yourself up over the little things—it'll only make you sick."*—Julianne, age 13

hurt when others treat you badly. When you stop to think about it, the only thing you have control over in the situation is your reaction, so keep your focus there. Learn to let go of the other things. You will achieve a lot more balance that way.

SUCCESS SECRET #25

Learn how to relax.

Perhaps the biggest part of managing your emotions, besides remembering what you can and can't control, is learning to relax. It is only when we are in a relaxed state that we can think clearly enough to discern what's inside the hula hoop from what's outside of our control. Furthermore, it is only when we are relaxed that we can get control of ourselves and our emotions.

Learning to relax requires you to know what it feels like when you are in a calm state, as well as what it feels like when you are not. They more you know about how *you* feel in these various states, the easier it is to teach yourself to be calm.

The easiest way to discover your own calm state is to define what it means to *not* be calm. Try watching an action-filled movie. Pay attention to how your body feels. Are you tense? Are your shoulders tight? What about your jaw?

After the movie is over, take stock of your feelings—physical and emotional. Are you tired? Does your body feel looser? Is there still tightness in your shoulders or jaw?

Try this a few times in different situations. After a while, you will be able to recognize both a calm and a not calm state of being.

Once you know what each state feels like, you must learn how to move from one state to the other. Using the Breathing Colors technique, taking a break, and counting to 10 are all ways you can learn to relax. Throughout the book I will list other ways you can learn to calm down.

Once you *think* you're calm, it is important to make sure. Stress and anxiety can be tricky, sneaking up you when you least expect it. The quiz below can help you learn how to ensure you are in a calm state.

QUIZ: AM I RELAXED?

Directions: Circle your answer for each question.

1. Do you have any tension in your body, especially in places like your back, your shoulders, and your jaw?

   YES   NO

2. Is your breathing fast?

   YES   NO

3. Do you feel hyper-focused and "ready for action"?

   YES   NO

4. Are you feeling super happy or super sad?

   YES   NO

5. Do you feel like you are ready to explode?

   YES   NO

Too many yes answers on this quiz means you are not relaxed. Try a few deep breaths and taking a break. When you're done, ask yourself these questions again.

SUCCESS SECRET #26

Embrace your intensity.

Being intense in thinking, in your physical reactions to things, and in your emotions is not a bad thing. In fact, it is the very thing that can make you excel. If you think of it differently, intensity is just another word for passion. Passion is what drives the artist to create, the doctor to find a cure, the teacher to teach, and you to learn. Passion is a very good thing. So, embrace your passion and your intensity—it is one of the very best parts of *you*.

> *"Like it or not, I know that I am a pretty intense person. I might as well figure out how to deal with it."—Peter, age 12*

Parents Sound Off

Parents have a sense of your emotions. They know how hard it can be to manage and control the turbulent wave of feelings that you sometimes experience. Talk to your parents about their thoughts regarding your emotions. Do their comments look like these?

» "(My child) is intensely connected with the world, her friends, and family."—Kathy

» "Just my prodding to get (my child) to talk is enough to make her upset and start crying, like she assumes there must be something wrong if I'm prodding her about it."—Sato

» "Sometimes it is so hard to know how to help my children with their emotions. They are so hard on themselves, so explosive, so sensitive—some days just saying 'Hi' is enough to set them off."—Erica

» "Dealing with my child when she shuts down is so hard. Nothing I say seems to help. I worry about her self-esteem over the long run as I watch her struggle to manage her emotions."—Lara

Remembering that your parents are your allies when it comes to learning about your emotions can be difficult. Take a moment to talk with them about their feelings. Together you can not only learn to manage your intensity, but embrace it as well.

Managing your emotions may be one of the hardest things you learn in this journey of discovering the deeper you, but it is also one of the most rewarding. By learning all of the wonderful things your emotions are telling you and facing each feeling with bravery and confidence, you will learn to be the master of your passions—and you will go far!

What Do You Think?

It's time for you to reflect on your feelings and what they mean to you. Take a few moments and think about these questions.

HOW DO YOU DEMONSTRATE YOUR EMOTIONAL INTENSITY? IS IT SOMETHING THAT BOTHERS YOU AT ALL?

WHAT ARE THE BEST WAYS FOR YOU TO CALM DOWN AND RELAX?

WHAT ARE YOUR TRICKS FOR MANAGING YOUR FEELINGS?

Part II

You spend more than half of your life either at school or doing school-related things. Homework, tests, projects—it's all part of the school experience. For gifted kids, this is both a good thing and a bad thing.

Hardwired to learn easily, some of you excel at school—pushing yourselves to achieve consistently. Others of you do only what you need to get by. Still others of you struggle. Whether you are a high-achieving gifted kid or one who struggles, you are all likely to experience both highs and lows when it comes to school. The next few chapters will cover the most typical problems that arise in your school experience: homework mishaps, perfectionism, and the pressure to perform.

Let's start off with a little quiz to test your knowledge about academics and giftedness. Hang on to your answers for now, but be sure to come back after reading this section to see if any of your answers have changed.

QUIZ: GIFTEDNESS AND SCHOOL

Directions: Circle your answer for each question.

1. Being gifted means homework should not take very long.

   TRUE   FALSE

2. Mistakes mean I am not as smart as I thought I was.

   TRUE   FALSE

3. Because I'm gifted, I don't need to study as much as most people.

   TRUE   FALSE

4. There is nothing I can do about the pressure I feel at school.

   TRUE   FALSE

5. Because I'm gifted, my teachers should expect that I will do well.

   TRUE   FALSE

Chapter 4

> *"People always assume that GATE kids can do everything really well, even when you may struggle."—Kevin, age 13*

Most people assume that gifted kids have it easy in school. You know this isn't always true, understanding that the routine nature of school can make it boring to you. Repetitive assignments often feel like torture, and minutes of simple work can easily turn into hours.

One of the biggest issues all school-aged children face is with homework—the task that many parents and children dread. Instead of simply being practice for the concepts taught in school, homework has turned into a battle zone for many households—maybe even yours.

The problem with homework and gifted kids usually boils down to this: Homework is repetitive, rote work that many of you have already mastered, or it is vague and filled with open-ended questions that you aren't certain you understand clearly. The result in both situations is the same: Work that was designed to be a quick and simple review of concepts taught in school turns into an ordeal that is typically filled with strong emotional reactions. You and your parents are often left feeling frustrated, angry, and exhausted.

The tips throughout this chapter address ways to streamline homework. Hopefully, after reading this chapter, you will find homework less of a chore and be able to create more time to spend with your friends and family.

SUCCESS SECRET #27

Start with the easy stuff.

Have you ever sat down to do your homework, only to find you were confused on the very first thing you attempted? Moments like these are enough to turn homework time into a nightmare. Instead of getting frustrated and spending hours on the things that confuse you, why not

"I like to get the easy stuff out of the way first, before I work on stuff that takes longer."—Maka, age 9

skip ahead to something easy? In fact, go through your work and get all of the easy, fast stuff out of the way. Make a list of questions on the harder things that confuse you. Once you relax, you will likely find that you understand a lot more than you realize. Try it out the next time you find yourself frustrated with your homework. My guess is that you'll get through the work a lot faster.

SUCCESS SECRET #28

Always give 100%.

Sometimes gifted kids assume that because they are smart and most things come very easily to them, homework will be a breeze. You may feel this way as well. The truth is, being smart isn't enough to have success in school. It also takes discipline, self-control, and commitment.

"Just because you are gifted, doesn't mean you shouldn't work hard."—Leif, age 13

This is especially true when it comes to homework.

When things come easily to you, it is natural to want to kick back and let things slide. Over time, you may stop giving schoolwork your all and settle for less than you are capable of. Eventually, giving less than 100% becomes a habit. Giving less than 80% can become a habit as well. And, sooner or later, you may stop caring altogether.

What happens when things get harder, which they always do at some point? What then? If you're already in the habit of giving less than your best, then you will struggle when things get harder. Confronted with difficult work without the necessary work habits to persevere can leave you feeling like a failure—and all because you became comfortable with giving less than your best.

I don't know about you, but that seems like a very bad plan to me.

The easiest way to fix the problem is to never settle for less than your very best. Give 100% in everything you do and try. That way when things get hard, you will have the necessary drive and perseverance to push through the difficult work until it becomes easy.

SUCCESS SECRET #29

Homework is not a race.

You come home from school on a beautiful afternoon. Your friends are bugging you to come out and play. They don't have the same diligence you do about your homework. They seldom get it done. Instead, they spend their afternoons playing ball in the neighborhood, skateboarding, or playing the latest video games.

You try to persuade your parents to let you go play for an hour, saying you'll finish your homework when you get back. But, they say no. "The rule is you must finish your homework before you play," they say.

> "Try hard to do your homework thoroughly. Otherwise, you'll just wind up having to do it over. That's what has happened to me."—Janie, age 11

So, you do the only thing that makes sense to you at the time . . .

You rush through your work and dash out to meet your friends.

In your hurry, you forget to check it over. You forget to make sure you've finished everything—something your teacher points out to you the next day, just before she calls your mom.

Darn. Another bad plan.

Homework is not a race. In fact, schoolwork is not a race. Few things in life really are. Homework is about getting the needed practice to be able to prove you've mastered certain concepts. It's also about learning *how* to be responsible.

Fortunately, you're smart. Most of your work will take you less time to complete than it takes other people if you don't get stressed, overwhelmed, or bored.

So, next time, don't race through your work. Take a breath, give it 100%, and try to keep yourself from getting emotionally overwhelmed by the work—whether it is boring or hard. You will find that it takes less time in the long run to do it right the first time.

SUCCESS SECRET #30 **Find a quiet place to do homework.**

One of the keys to homework success is finding the right place to do homework. The kitchen table, a desk in your room, and the library are all good places to work. The key is to limit distractions. Look for a place that has good lighting, limited noise, and a table to work at with a comfortable, but not too comfortable, chair. You want it to feel like school in the sense that you're supposed to work, not play. If the area you choose is too comfortable, you will find yourself very easily distracted, and finishing your homework may turn into a nightmare.

Another thing to look for when choosing your ideal homework spot is the availability of your supplies. Do you have paper, pens, pencils, highlighters, and anything else you need to complete your homework?

For some of you, your options for where to complete your assignments may be limited. Perhaps you go to a friend's house after school and he doesn't start his homework until after you leave. Or perhaps you have to go to your parent's office to complete your homework. Whatever the circumstances are, you need to find the best place for you to get your things done—one that you can identify as a place where you complete homework.

Once you have the "where" figured out, I want you to collect the most common items you need for completing your work, and make sure they are available where you need them. If your homework spot varies, then put what you need in your backpack so you have it handy.

Ultimately, homework management is your responsibility, so find a place to work that makes it easier to get it done. Take a few minutes and complete the worksheet below about the best places for you to work. Once you're done, go over it with your parents and make sure they approve. They may have different ideas regarding the best place and time for you to work. Listen to what they have to say and reach an agreement together.

THE BEST PLACES TO COMPLETE MY HOMEWORK

1. List three ideas for homework places, keeping in mind the things discussed in this section.

    a. First choice: _____

    b. Second choice: _____

    c. Third choice: _____

2. Review the list with your parents. Do you need to make any changes to it?

3. Make a list of the supplies you may need to complete your homework. I've listed a few to get you started.
    a. Pencil and eraser
    b. Paper

    c. _____

    d. _____

    e. _____

4. Gather the items and store them near your place to work or in your backpack, depending on your particular situation.
5. Now you're ready to get to work!

SUCCESS SECRET #31

Make sure you understand your work before you leave school.

There is nothing worse than sitting down to start your work and realizing that you don't understand what the teacher wanted you to do. This is particularly true if you've completed Success Secret #27 and finished the easy things already, leaving you with only the hard stuff. Now what?

You could ask your parents or call a friend. Both solutions would work. There is a better one you can try first—one that will reduce the number of times you come home confused about your school work.

Make sure you know what you need to do *before* you leave school.

Developing this habit can be hard and even uncomfortable. It will require you to ask questions and maybe even admit when you are unsure about an assignment—something no gifted kid wants to do. But remember, your teachers are there to help you. They do not expect you to understand everything they're saying all of the time. No one expects that of you, except maybe you. What is expected is that you will ask questions when you are uncertain of something.

How do you know when you are unsure? I know, it seems like a silly question to ask. In my experience, most gifted kids don't realize they're uncertain about something until after they get home and attempt the assignment. The following list is designed to help you make sure that you are clear about your assignments.

QUESTIONS TO ASK YOURSELF

1. Do you have each assignment written down on a calendar or planner?
2. Do you know exactly what is required to complete each task?
3. Do you have the necessary information to complete each task?
4. Do you know when each assignment is due?
5. Do you know what and/or how the work is being graded?

There are many other questions you can list for yourself, but these will get you started. Knowing how to answer them should enable you to complete every assigned task that comes home.

SUCCESS SECRET #32

Make a plan to complete your work.

In addition to having a place to work and knowing exactly what to work on, designing a nightly homework plan is another way to guarantee a night free from any homework drama. A homework plan is just another name for a to-do list. List everything that needs to be completed and the order in which you will finish it. If there are long-term projects or upcoming tests, be sure to include them on your list. (Yes, you should study and/or work on projects throughout the entire time given, not just the night before they are due).

Once you know what to work on, list the items in order of completion. Like I mentioned earlier, start with something you can finish quickly. This will give you an immediate sense of accomplishment and will motivate you to continue to work. Alternating easy tasks that can be completed quickly with harder tasks is another thing to consider when setting up your homework plan.

On nights when you have a lot to complete, it is important to schedule breaks. Similarly, if you are involved in sports or other activities after school, you will want to schedule them into your overall homework plan as well.

Some nights you will find that there is very little to complete. This is when you can get a head start on your projects or tests. By utilizing your time wisely each week, you can keep yourself from becoming too overwhelmed on long nights.

TIPS FOR MAKING A HOMEWORK PLAN

1. Look over your planner and make a list of everything that you need to complete that night for homework.
2. Add projects, long-term assignments, and studying for tests. The next Success Secret will give you ideas on planning those things out each week.
3. Add any extracurricular activities or breaks you will need in the nightly schedule.
4. Once you have a complete list, rearrange it in the order in which you want to complete tasks. If you tend to procrastinate or take a long time to do simple things, give yourself a timeframe for completing the work.
5. Be sure to cross things off as you finish them. This will help you *see* all of the work you are completing.

SUCCESS SECRET #33

Don't put off your projects.

Projects, weekly assignments, and long-term tests are the things most gifted kids tend to overlook when planning out their homework. I can understand why: If it isn't due right away, then you tend to forget about it. Plus, it's easy to forget to write it down as part of your homework.

> *"Waiting to the last minute to do your work only makes you more stressed. Try to get things done early. You'll sleep better."—Chandler, age 13*

Here's the problem with that: Although you may work quickly and need to study less than someone who is not gifted, you will easily become overwhelmed if you leave things until the last minute.

The solution? Plan out all of the tasks that aren't due the following day. This includes projects, weekly homework packets, tests, and anything else that you have multiple days to complete. The easiest way to get this done is to break the task down into small parts. If it's a weekly homework packet, decide which pages you will complete each night to make sure the packet is done on time. If it's a test, then decide which things you will study each night and how you'll study. (Will you review your notes? Use flashcards?) If it's a project, then break down the task into smaller ones—research, writing, assembling the project itself—and decide which part you are doing each night.

Many of you will have teachers or parents that break this stuff down for you. Although it's wonderful that they are willing to do that, the responsibility is ultimately yours. You are the one in school. You are the one earning the grades. Eventually, when you move into higher grades, your teachers and parents won't break your assignments down for you. So, the sooner you learn how to do it, the better.

After you have broken down the various tasks, write what you are going to achieve each day in your planner or on a calendar. When it is time to draft a nightly homework plan, be sure to include these items on your list.

Breaking down tasks and making lists is a great way to keep your homework under control and maintain your emotional balance—no matter how busy you may feel.

SUCCESS SECRET #34 Know who you can call if you get stuck.

Sometimes things go wrong despite your best efforts to write things down and make a plan. Maybe you lose your planner, you're not at school, or you just forgot to make sure you were prepared. Hey, it happens to everyone sooner or later. The important thing to remember is to stay calm and have a Plan B—an emergency plan.

Emergency plans are just that—your plan for what to do when things go wrong. You still have to complete your work, even when things go bad. So how are you going to do that when you don't have any idea of what to do?

This is when you need to call a friend, look up the homework on the school's website, or figure out another way to get the job done. Part of being a successful student means knowing how to navigate through an emergency when it happens.

Make a list of all of the ways you can get answers to homework questions. Think about the ways your school offers help for students who have forgotten their homework, as well as which friends may have the information you need. Keep a few copies of this list in important places, including your backpack, your homework study space, with your parents, and near the phone.

Emergencies will always happen. Being prepared can keep the emergency from turning into a disaster.

MY HOMEWORK EMERGENCY LIST

1. What methods does your school offer for finding out about homework in an emergency? I've listed a few that may apply. Cross out the ones your school does not offer, and list others I may have left off.
   a. Homework hotline
   b. School website
   c. Teacher website

   d. _____

   e. _____

2. List at least three friends who may know the homework for the night. If you have multiple teachers, try to list at least three friends for each teacher and class.

Friend	Class	Phone Number

3. Ask your friends for a phone number so you can call in an emergency. Be sure to make sure your parents are OK with you getting or giving out your phone number *before* you complete this step.

4. Brainstorm other possible homework emergency solutions with your parents. Write down your most feasible ideas.

_____

_____

_____

5. Remember to keep copies of your list in several places, including:
   a. in your backpack,
   b. in your homework study space, and
   c. near the phone.

Parents Sound Off

Parents are as frustrated as you are when it comes to homework. They express concern about the time it takes to complete homework, the emotional drama that often happens when students get overwhelmed, and the stress they feel from you. At the same time, parents understand the role homework plays in helping you build responsibility. The quotes below express some of their concerns and feelings about homework time.

» "Homework that is repetitive and goes nowhere, and the notion that she needs to do everything perfectly and on time, is difficult and frustrating for her."—Yeida

» "Homework time can be a nightmare in our house. Other times it is no problem at all. It just depends on what the kids have going on, how tired we all are, and whether or not they understand the work."—Jonathan

» "Homework is 'busy work' and she doesn't enjoy doing it, but we can make it more challenging for her by just asking her more difficult questions"—Thomas

» "Homework is a challenge for my daughter, who insists on going above and beyond in her work and producing perfect handwriting every time. This can make homework take a long time to finish."—Tiare

Ask your parents if these quotes reflect some of the ways they feel. What can you do together to make homework less of a nightmare in your home?

Overall, homework is a necessary part of life. It provides practice for upcoming measures of mastery and teaches aspects of responsibility you will need as an adult. Using the tips suggested throughout this chapter can make homework time less of a chore and enable you to get it done quickly and efficiently.

What Do You Think?

Take a few minutes and think about your feelings regarding homework, then answer the questions on the next page. Talk with your parents about some of these things too. Homework time doesn't need to be filled with drama.

HOW LONG DOES IT TAKE YOU TO FINISH YOUR HOMEWORK (ON AVERAGE)? DO YOU THINK THIS IS A LONG TIME OR A SHORT TIME, COMPARED TO YOUR FRIENDS?

WHAT IS THE HARDEST PART OF HOMEWORK TIME? THE WORKLOAD? THE BOREDOM FACTOR? THE PLANNING ASPECT?

HOW CAN YOU SOLVE THE PROBLEMS LISTED ABOVE? DISCUSS THESE SOLUTIONS WITH YOUR PARENTS AND TURN HOMEWORK TIME INTO SOMETHING PRODUCTIVE AND NOT SOMETHING THAT IS FILLED WITH ARGUMENTS OR TEARS.

Chapter 5

> *"I hate it when I do poorly on something in school. I mean, I'm smart. I'm in a gifted program—so things are supposed to come easily for me. If it doesn't, than how could I really be smart, right?"—Ryan, age 9*

I have a question for you—do you tend to measure how smart you are in terms of how easy everything is? I bet you do. In fact, you probably also believe that long, complicated assignments that you have a hard time with are either bad assignments (the teacher messed up) or proof that you are not really as smart as everyone thinks you are.

Actually, neither assumption is true. Your intellectual abilities and your school performance seldom relate directly to one another. Yes, it's true that most assignments will come more easily to you because you are smart. But, if your teacher is doing a good job in challenging you, you should find yourself having to really work on some things in class. Believing that working hard in school means you aren't smart is a false assumption and something you will need to change if you are going to reach your potential.

Assignments can seem hard for a few reasons, many of them related to the attributes of giftedness we've already discussed. For example, sometimes an assignment seems a lot harder than the teacher meant it to be. Why? Because you read too much into the assignment. You are overthinking it. You believed the teacher was asking you for something far more complicated than was intended. This can lead to endless hours of work and a lot of emotional angst.

SUCCESS SECRET #35

Don't overthink things.

As I already mentioned, it is very easy for gifted kids to overthink things. This usually happens because your brain is working so hard and fast all of the time. As a result, you often think things are more complex than they are, believing that nothing can be as easy as it seems to you. You are always looking for the trick.

> *"My brain is always thinking about a million different things."—Maddy, age 13*

Guess what? There rarely is a trick. Sometimes the easy answer really is the answer.

Let me give you an example of how you may be overthinking things. Let's say the teacher gives an assignment to write a short paragraph stating the color of the sky. Most students will go home and write a few sentences that basically say the color of the sky is blue.

Not you—you will struggle with the assignment, wondering what time of day you're supposed to look at the sky, whether or not there are any clouds, or what the moisture content of the atmosphere is at that time. Because you did not get clarification on the assignment, you will think and think and think—trying to riddle out what the teacher is actually looking for.

This may take hours and many, many tears.

In the end, you will likely write several pages explaining how you can't possibly answer the question without knowing more information. What do you think the teacher actually wanted? That's right—a few sentences saying the sky is blue.

Overthinking without getting clarification will almost always lead to more frustration. Think about that the next time you begin to spin and decide if it's really worth it.

SUCCESS SECRET #36   Accepting help is a smart thing to do.

Overthinking is really only a problem when you don't seek clarification—when you don't ask for help. But, sometimes, help is offered even when you don't ask, and sometimes, you really *need* the help. Yet, as with most gifted kids, you are reluctant to accept help, thinking it makes you look less gifted somehow. Or, maybe you think that accepting help makes you less perfect—an idea that may cause literal pain.

The truth is that everyone needs help from time to time. Accepting it when it is offered is the key to making the most of your giftedness. No one really expects you to know everything all of the time. So, when your teachers offer clarification or your parents offer help, hear them out. You may learn an unexpected tip that makes everything a lot easier for you. Even if you don't learn anything this time, you are opening yourself up to future learning—and that is always a smart thing to do.

> *"Teachers are there to help you. Don't shut them out. It won't help." —Jin, age 11*

SUCCESS SECRET #37

There are many ways to learn information.

Part of understanding yourself and reaching your potential involves understanding how *you* best learn information. Do you prefer to listen to your teachers? Are you visual, seeing words as pictures in your head? Are you more hands-on, preferring to touch and manipulate things as a way to learn? Take the short quiz below to help determine your main way of learning. Use this information to help you make the most of your school experiences.

QUIZ: HOW DO YOU LEARN?

Directions: Circle your answer for each question.

1. I learn best when I can see a picture of something.

   TRUE   **FALSE**

2. I like to build things.

   TRUE   **FALSE**

3. I talk a lot about my day and really like to listen to other people talking.

   TRUE   **FALSE**

4. When my teacher is talking, I make pictures of the words in my head—it makes remembering things easier.

   TRUE   **FALSE**

5. If I write things down, I remember them better—even when I don't study.

TRUE   FALSE

6. I understand a story that I hear better than a story that I read.

TRUE   FALSE

7. When I study vocabulary words, I like to make a picture of the word or concept. It helps me remember them better.

TRUE   FALSE

8. Using blocks for math and sentence strips for writing really helps me remember things.

TRUE   FALSE

9. I spell words out loud when I am studying—that way I remember them better.

TRUE   FALSE

Go through and look at your answers. True on numbers 1, 4, and 7 means you learn best by seeing things. True on 2, 5, and 8 means you need to use your hands and touch things to learn best. And true on 3, 6, and 9 means listening to information is your best way of learning. Some of you will find that you answered true to questions for each of the areas. This means you are a multimodal learner.

There are lots of other ways to learn and lots of other tools to discover just what kind of learner you truly are. The important thing is to begin to understand how you learn best.

SUCCESS SECRET #38

When in doubt, ask.

Ah yes, asking questions—the most difficult thing in the world for many gifted kids. Most of you will avoid it completely, deciding to figure out something on your own rather than asking a question and appearing like you don't have all of the answers after all.

The reality is, taking three times longer to do something because you were afraid to seek clarification is sillier than appearing like you need help—a lot sillier. You've probably heard the statement "There are no stupid questions except the ones not asked"—this is exactly what we are talking about here. You must be willing to risk appearing foolish if you are going to learn. And this means you must ask questions.

Why? If for no other reason than to make sure you understand what you are being asked to do. Oftentimes gifted kids stress out over assignments simply because they got home without knowing what the teacher wanted from them. Had they asked, there would have been no confusion, and homework time would have gone more smoothly.

> "Be willing to talk to your teachers and ask for help on things, even if the other kids in the class laugh." —Erika, age 11

So, do yourself a favor the next time you are uncertain about something—an assignment in school or a chore at home—and ask questions. Keep asking until you understand what you are supposed to be doing. If you don't ask, everyone will assume you understand things and will expect you to be able to do the work assigned.

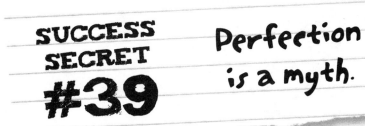

SUCCESS SECRET #39 — Perfection is a myth.

Perfectionism is the need to be or appear perfect in everything you do, never making a mistake on anything. And, it's totally unrealistic. No one is perfect, and striving for constant perfection is the quickest way to getting yourself overwhelmed, especially on your schoolwork.

Although trying your best is a good thing, believing that there is no room for error is a mistake most gifted kids (and adults) make every single day. In the constant pursuit of perfection, kids like you may become afraid to take risks in school, decide not to turn in their work to the teacher for fear that it isn't good enough, or simply become too overwhelmed to even attend school.

So, why do you fall into the perfectionism trap? Most of the time it has to do with your belief that everyone else thinks you have to be perfect if you are gifted. You worry that mistakes will disappoint your teachers, your parents, even your friends. And as a result, you allow yourself to believe that the only way to make sure you don't disappoint anyone is to be perfect.

Man, that's an impossible task to give yourself. No wonder you and other gifted kids feel so much stress most of the time.

A better way to deal with the pressures of being gifted is to remember that learning is a process. Your parents know this, as do your teachers. They really don't expect you to know everything instantly. They understand that learning takes time and that it is through your mistakes that a deeper understanding of things occurs.

Teachers and parents will often sit with kids when a mistake is made and re-explain the lessons being taught. The problem is, you may look at this as if they are disappointed. Nothing is further from the truth. They're just trying to guide you to knowledge—teach you how to look at your mistakes as opportunities to grow. Trust me, they aren't expecting you to be perfect and know everything.

TIPS FOR BEATING THE PERFECTIONISM TRAP

1. Make of list of the things you think need to be perfect (i.e., homework, answers on tests).
2. Set goals for yourself regarding homework and other things. Ask yourself if the goals are realistic to achieve. Show them to your parents or teachers to make sure they are reasonable.
3. Focus on the process of learning, not the grades.
4. Practice the PROOF technique in Success Secret #10. Use it as a way to help you make sure you are looking at the situation realistically.
5. Ask yourself these questions whenever you are getting stressed about making mistakes:
   a. Is what I am feeling realistic? (Use the PROOF technique to find out.)
   b. Are my goals reasonable?
   c. What would happen if I failed?
   d. Can I change how I am feeling? (Remember the Hula Hoop technique.)

Go through these tips frequently until you've made a habit of working past your perfectionism tendencies.

SUCCESS SECRET #40 — Mistakes are opportunities to learn.

Speaking of mistakes as opportunities to learn, did you know that many of the things we use every day were discovered or invented as a direct result of a mistake? It's true. By taking risks and trying new things, you will often make mistakes. Sometimes those mistakes can lead to amazing discoveries and enable you to think of new things that you never considered before. But, if you aren't willing to take a risk, if you get too stuck on your perfectionism to be willing to make a mistake, you may be missing out on an amazing opportunity to learn something new.

Take a look at the list on the next page—everything on it was discovered by accident, either when a scientist was looking for something else or when someone was just messing around. Amazing, right? Where would we be without the accidental discovery of the Americas, the medicine we use for diabetes, or even sticky notes?

Be willing to take risks, and who knows—maybe your mistakes will lead to a great invention too.

AMAZING DISCOVERIES THAT CAME FROM MISTAKES

1. Christopher Columbus was actually looking for Asia when he found the New World.
2. Medicines including penicillin, the smallpox vaccine, and Coumadin, all widely used now, were discovered by scientists who were looking for other things (Banner, 2008).
3. A cook in China discovered fireworks when he accidentally mixed three common kitchen items (HowStuffWorks, 2007).
4. Play-Doh was created by accident when Noah and Joseph McVicker were trying to make wallpaper cleaner. It was later sold to a toy company (HowStuffWorks, 2007).
5. Post-It Notes were conceived by Arthur Fry as a way to keep bookmarks in hymnals and combined with an accidental invention of an adhesive made by 3M employee Spencer Silver (HowStuffWorks, 2007).

Quite an amazing list, isn't it? Without taking risks and being willing to fail, most of these things would have never been discovered or created.

SUCCESS SECRET #41 Listen to other people's suggestions.

As a kid, even a gifted kid, you have a lot of people offering advice: your teachers, your parents, your siblings, and maybe even your friends. It can be really hard to listen to all of these people. You have your own way of doing things. You know what the assignment is and how you think it should be done.

But, you don't know everything. Sometimes the advice from your parents can help you be better organized. Sometimes the advice from your siblings can keep you out of trouble. And sometimes the advice from teachers can save you hours of work.

Listening to other people's suggestions does not diminish you—it doesn't mean that you don't know things, nor does it mean that you're wrong. All it shows is a willingness on your part to see a different point a view. A willingness to learn.

> *"Always listen to your teachers, no matter how boring they may seem. Their words will help you later on."—Katelyn, age 13*

Trust me, to your teachers, parents, and siblings, being willing to hear something new is definitely a sign of being smart.

SUCCESS SECRET #42 — Take the time to think through a difficult problem.

Do you have a hard time working through difficult problems? I know a lot of gifted children who do. Maybe it's because it is scary to face a hard problem and the idea that you could fail. Maybe it has to do with the horrible feeling you can get in the pit of your stomach when you're confronted with something you don't instinctively know how to do. And, maybe it's because you'll avoid that stuck feeling at all costs, even if it means blowing off something that you really should do.

Regardless of your reasons, solving difficult problems can be one of the most difficult things about the world of school. Take a look at the tips on the next page and try them the next time you get stuck.

TIPS FOR SOLVING PROBLEMS

1. First you must relax. Practice the relaxation strategies from Chapter 2.
2. Read through the question carefully. Make notes, if needed, about what the question is asking.
3. Brainstorm solutions. Evaluate your solutions to see if they work and make logical sense.
4. Pick a solution and apply it to the problem. If it doesn't work, repeat the process with a different solution.
5. When in doubt, ask for help.

SUCCESS SECRET #43

Learning new information does not mean you are dumb.

I remember when my oldest daughter was starting third grade. She was so angry with me for not teaching her everything she needed to learn before the year started. She hated learning new things at school. She always felt like she should already know everything. When she realized she didn't, she would get frustrated.

I bet you feel that way at times too. It's one of those things related to being

> *"I get very frustrated when I don't understand something I'm being taught for the first time, even though I know it's OK not to understand some things."*
> —Maya, age 14

gifted—the feeling that if you are really as smart as everyone thinks you are, you *should* already know everything about everything.

In your mind, you know this isn't true. But, in your heart, you can't help it—you really feel like learning new things means you're not smart. It's hard to change that belief, it really is, but remember this: Remaining open to learning new things is one of the smartest things you will ever do in your life. It will enable you to make new discoveries about yourself, the subjects you are studying, and even the world. So try to stay as open-minded as you can . . . and when that little voice in your head tries to convince you that you *should* already know everything, learn to ignore it.

Parents Sound Off

Parents have a hard time dealing with your perfectionism too, as well as the stress you show related to that perfectionism. Check out what they think—it may make their reactions to your feelings more understandable.

» "(My child) gets frustrated—she is a perfectionist and gets mad if things aren't completely perfect and on time." —James

» "Thank goodness my kids and I are all gifted—it makes understanding their stress over school so much easier for me."—Asya

» "Oh yeah, my daughter is definitely a perfectionist. Not just in her schoolwork but in all aspects of her life—school, her room, sports. It can be exhausting."—Gloria

» "It can be WWIII at our house when my kids are in their 'perfectionist' moods. No matter what my wife and I tell them, they just turn themselves into a mess."—Doug

Perfectionism and stress have the power to spin any household into chaos. Take a moment and ask your parents what they think about your perfectionism issues. Did you learn anything new?

The need to excel is nothing new for most gifted kids. But, this need to excel can be the very thing that inhibits some kids from reaching their full potential. The stress, the refusal to take risks, and the perfectionism—all of these attributes work against your potential. Look at the section on the next page. Revisit the questions often as you discover what you really feel about your abilities in school and in life.

What Do You Think?

Reflect on the following questions, being as honest as you can. What are your areas of difficulty when it comes to reaching your potential?

DO YOU STRUGGLE WITH
TRYING TO BE PERFECT? WHAT
STRATEGIES CAN YOU TRY TO
MINIMIZE YOUR PERFECTIONISM?

THINK ABOUT A RECENT
MISTAKE YOU MADE AT SCHOOL.
WHAT WAS IT? HOW DID YOU
DEAL WITH THE MISTAKE?

DO YOU GET FRUSTRATED LEARNING
NEW THINGS? WHY? HOW CAN
YOU CHANGE YOUR REACTIONS?

Chapter 6

> "I am really hard on myself. I expect that I am supposed to be perfect in everything. So if I'm not, I can't really handle it. I know that I shouldn't feel that way, but yeah, I am struggling with that. Still." —Rebecca, age 13

Being gifted comes with a lot of expectations—from parents, from friends, and from the world. But, nothing compares to the expectations you put on yourself: everything from thinking about grades ("Only straight A's will do"), to thinking about world problems ("I must keep global warming from killing off the polar bears"), to wondering about your future ("How many activities should I be in so I can get into a great college?"). It's enough to make anyone a bit sick.

Part of this pressure comes from the wide-angle view of life that is natural for a gifted child. You get the bigger picture on things such as understanding world issues, the impact of grades on future endeavors, and the need for a good education.

You also may add to this pressure unnecessarily. You think that your teacher's questions about the few mistakes you made on a test are signs that she expects perfection. You assume that your parents' constant inquiries regarding your homework and grades mean they demand straight A's. You even think your friends will be disappointed if you aren't constantly successful.

Want to know a secret? Most of the pressure is a myth. You're doing it to yourself. Don't get me wrong: Some pressure is a good thing. It can keep you focused and provide the motivation you need to excel. However, in its extreme it will work against you, causing you to fold into an emotional mess.

SUCCESS SECRET #44

Take it easy on yourself.

I don't know about you, but most of the gifted kids I've talked to are really hard on themselves. They demand perfection and precision in all tasks. When they make a mistake or earn a grade lower than they want, they work even harder the next time. They are driven and intense in all aspects of their lives.

And, they never ease up.

Approaching life that way is not necessarily a bad thing. Anything taken to extremes can be too hard to manage. Putting constant pressure on yourself will throw you into an emotional cycle that can be very hard to break. Remember, you aren't just intense when it comes to academic performance. You are passionate in all aspects of your life, especially when it comes to your feelings.

> *"You're going to make mistakes sometimes. When that happens, try to learn from it—don't beat yourself up. That never helps anything."—Sydney, age 13*

Learning to give yourself permission to make a mistake, to fail, is the first step in learning to control the impact of the pressure you put on yourself. It is the key to everything else. So the next time you are mentally beating yourself up for making a mistake or failing at something, try to remember that the mistake really doesn't define you as a person.

It is just a mistake.

SUCCESS SECRET #45
Stress never solved a problem.

Stress is an interesting thing. It can be the force that drives our bodies to respond to a crisis, enabling us to escape a dangerous situation. But, it can also be paralyzing, making us unable to complete the simplest of things.

Stress is connected to the "fight or flight" response our bodies make in times of an emergency and is a necessary part of biology, *except* when it takes over our lives. Stress, taken in the extreme, can force you into that fight or flight response for too long and that causes a lot of problems.

One of the biggest problems involves our brains. You see, your stress response, or the fight or flight response, is designed to slow down the part of your brain that thinks and solves problems, diverting energy to the part of your body that can get you out of the situation quickly and safely. Let's think about that for a minute: When you are stressed, you literally can't think and analyze clearly.

Wow! No wonder it is hard to solve problems when you are stressed.

Now this fight or flight response was designed to be short term. Sadly, most of us get stuck in our stress, reliving the things that stress us out over and over and over again. Our brain reacts the same way each and every time—it slows down its thinking.

Hmm. I don't know about you, but that seems like a bad plan to me.

The best way to stop all of this? Stop stressing.

> "You have to put your stress aside sometimes, and just focus on getting all of your work done."—Bishar, age 13

SUCCESS SECRET #46
Remember to take breaks.

OK, you know you need to stop stressing about things. How do you do this? We've talked about some strategies in Part I already like deep breathing and taking care of yourself.

Taking breaks is another way to stop your stress cycle and enable your brain to start thinking clearly again. Although there is really no *wrong* way to take a break, some things can make the break more productive in terms of making sure you are letting go of your stress.

TIPS FOR TAKING BREAKS THE SMART WAY

1. Take breaks when you feel your own stress cycle beginning—the sooner the better.
2. If you catch your stress early, try taking deep breaths or using other relaxation strategies to calm down your thoughts.
3. Go back to work as soon as you are calm. Repeat the relaxation technique each time you feel your stress rise.
4. Don't let your breaks become an excuse to not complete your work. Breaks are only to help you relax and refocus.
5. Some people control stress and pressure best when they schedule breaks into their work time. For example, plan on working for 30 minutes and then taking a 5-minute stretch break. Use a timer to keep yourself honest.

SUCCESS SECRET #47

Grades aren't everything.

Yep, I said it. Grades are *not* everything. I know, I know, you really want to argue that point with me. You want to convince me that without grades there will be no success later on, no proof of how smart you are. You want to say that grades are the things your parents and teachers think about most. I know.

I am still going to say it: Grades are only a piece of the picture—one little piece.

The really important part of learning comes from the doing, the "how" behind the grade. Take math, for example. If everything was really about grades or the answers to things, your teacher wouldn't care whether or not you showed your work, only about whether or not you got the correct answer.

We both know that isn't how it works. Your teacher *does* care about *how* you got your answers, and she does expect you to show your work. She is looking for the process of your learning, not just the answer. She wants to make sure you understand how to get an answer. That's where the actually learning takes place. The other things—the answers—are the results of your learning.

Putting this back in terms of your grades, it means that the grades are only the result of your learning. The actual way in which you learned the material—the how—is more important than the grades in the long run.

This is not to say you shouldn't care at all about grades. I know you do. It just means that they are not the only thing on which you should focus.

> *"I know I shouldn't care about grades, but I do. So I make sure to check everything at least twice before turning in a test or work."*—Pedro, age 9

SUCCESS SECRET #48 — You cannot think when you are frustrated.

Earlier, we talked about stress and how it impacts your ability to think. Guess what? The same applies to frustration. This is because feeling frustrated is another part of a stress response.

Frustration typically results when you feel disappointment in something or someone. It can happen when you try to do something and can't, like when you have a difficult problem on a test and can't figure it out, or when you try to explain something to someone and he doesn't understand you, no matter how hard you are trying. The feelings that arise in these situations can usually be defined as frustration.

> *"Freaking out before a test can make you do worse. I used to cry before tests, and it felt like I couldn't think right. It took a while, but I learned to get past it."—Tatianna, age 13*

Just like with stress, when you are frustrated you are not going to think clearly. Usually, you are going to get stuck in the frustration and have a hard time moving your thoughts to anything other than the feelings you have about the frustration, feelings that can include sadness, anger, and deep disappointment.

It is important to remember to relax as soon as you feel the frustration starting. Remind yourself that the feelings will pass if you remember to relax.

SUCCESS SECRET #49 The easiest way to perform better on a test is to relax.

You already know from the preceding Success Secrets that stress and frustration block your ability to think clearly. They also keep you from doing well on tests. In several studies, stress and test anxiety has been shown to inhibit concentration, memory, and focus (Cassady & Johnson, 2002). It can also impact your ability to read and comprehend material (Cassady, 2004).

Stress and test anxiety *really do* make tests more difficult. So, what can you do about it? Relax. Find ways to ease the test anxiety, and you will automatically improve your performance on tests.

TIPS FOR EASING TEST ANXIETY

1. Be prepared. Nothing makes you more relaxed than walking into the test knowing you studied.

2. If you don't understand a question, skip to one you can easily answer.

3. Once you've gone through the whole test and answered the questions you know, go back to the hard ones.

4. Take deep breaths and relax. Remember, you really can't think if you get too stressed and frustrated.

5. If you find yourself getting really worried before tests, try a little mental rehearsal:

    a. Imagine taking the test one step at a time—first you go into the class, then you get your pencil, then the teacher gives you the test, and so on.

b. Each time you feel stressed during your visualization, stop and take a few deep breaths until you are calm. Continue picturing the task.

c. Practice each step until you picture the entire test experience without stress.

Practice these skills regularly and you will quickly learn to master your test anxiety.

SUCCESS SECRET #50

Balance out the hard with the easy.

One of the tips I mentioned under Reducing Test Anxiety involved answering the easy questions on a test first. There is a reason for this—it is important for gifted kids to feel some success with working on tasks. This applies to both tests and the other work you do. If you only tackle the hard stuff, you will likely get frustrated to the point of giving up.

Balancing out the things that are hard for you to finish with the things that are easier is a great way to prevent this frustration overload. Start with something easy. Then do something harder. Alternate between easy and hard until everything is finished.

The other possibility is to complete everything that is easy first. This works particularly well on a test. But, with most work, alternating between easy and hard is actu-

"Being motivated to do the hard stuff can be so difficult at times. So can staying motivated to do the easy stuff. I guess motivation is just a hard thing."—Maria, age 11

ally better. It allows you to spread out the things that are going to give you the most difficulty.

Some days everything feels hard. This usually happens when you are struggling with your motivation. Maybe you are tired, or maybe you are overwhelmed. Either way, finding the desire to complete your work is hard.

On those days, it is essential to start with the easy things and build momentum. As you complete your tasks, crossing them off your to-do list, you will find your motivation returning. Before you know it, you will finish everything you had to do—without the tears and frustration that have occurred in the past.

SUCCESS SECRET #51 You are not your stress.

It is so hard not to define yourself by your feelings. The truth is that you are not your stress. Not at all.

The stress and frustration you feel are just a reaction to a situation you are experiencing. Like you learned with the Hula Hoop technique, you really have no control over what life throws your way. And although many of the things you experience at school—the pressure and expectations—may initially stress you out, you do have the ability to change your reactions. To do this, however, you must remember that stress, frustration, and the other things you feel are not the total of *who* you are.

Remembering this is pretty easy when you're calm. However, remembering it once you are stressed is a lot harder. The Truth About Me worksheet is designed to be a reminder about all of the great things you really are, especially during those times when you can't remember!

THE TRUTH ABOUT ME

1. List all of the positive things about you. Be sure to include things from the world of school, the world of friends, and the world of family. _____

    _____

    _____

2. Add some nice comments teachers and other adults have said about you. _____

    _____

    _____

3. List your goals and dreams for the future. _____

    _____

    _____

4. List your favorite things to do with friends and family.

    _____

    _____

5. After making your lists, take a minute and draw a picture, make a collage, create a soundtrack, or find another way to illustrate all of the great things you are. Keep the finished product someplace where you can refer to it often, or make several products so you have them at home and at school.

6. Remember to make a new list and a new picture or collage as you change. This way, you will always have a reminder handy of the truth about you as a person.

Parents Sound Off

Expectations and pressure are something parents have a lot of strong feelings about. Most of the things that you think are coming from your parents—pressure to get A's, the expectation that you should know how to do everything—your parents think come from you. Read their quotes and see for yourself just how differently you and your parents view this problem.

» "My kids think their teachers expect that everything they do will be perfect. Maybe the teachers do feel that way."—Janice

» "My kids impose more pressure on themselves than I ever could. In some ways that makes it easy on me. But I hate seeing what it does to them."—Nellie

» "My kids are both different in how the pressure they feel looks—my daughter tends to explode, whereas my son implodes. It makes me feel like I am walking on eggshells most of the time, just trying to not make them emotionally crack."—Kamari

» "Being confined by unnecessary limits . . . time, expectations, teacher's lack of knowledge or inability to answer difficult question . . . that is the most frustrating for all of us."—Shaun

Overall, although you and your parents both see and feel the pressure in your life, you often think differently about from where that pressure comes. It would be good to talk with your parents about your ideas and feelings. This will help all of you learn to manage pressure better.

Pressure, expectations, stress, and frustration—these are all realities in your life. Learning to manage these emotions will not only help you reach your potential, but it will give you the tools you will use as an adult to tackle similar feelings.

What Do You Think?

Now it's your turn to think about the pressure you may feel and what you can do about it. As with the other chapters, be sure to come back and reflect on these questions throughout the year. The pressures you feel today may not be the same ones you feel tomorrow.

WHAT PRESSURE DO YOU FEEL, AND HOW OFTEN DOES IT AFFECT YOU?

HOW CAN YOU WORK WITH THE PRESSURE IN ORDER TO REDUCE THE STRESS AND FRUSTRATION YOU MAY FEEL ABOUT SCHOOL?

HOW OFTEN DO YOU TAKE BREAKS, AND WHAT DO YOU DO DURING BREAKS? DO YOUR BREAKS HELP TO REDUCE YOUR FEELINGS OF FRUSTRATION REGARDING SCHOOL?

Part III

Relationships with friends can be a difficult thing for many gifted children. Hardwired to view things differently than most kids your age, you may struggle to find kids who understand your need for precision and logic or why you get so emotional over little things.

Those of you who do find friends with a similar view of life may still struggle, having to deal with the competition that commonly arises between gifted children. Maybe you struggle with being too intense for even your intense friends.

Whatever your issues may be, this section is designed to focus on the world of friends. Covering typical concerns like dealing with competition, being kind to one another, and learning how to embrace your differences, the next few chapters offer much-needed advice and tips for developing relationships that will bring out the best in all of you.

To start, let's see what you already know about gifted kids and friends. Remember to check back after you've read the entire section to see if anything has changed.

THE WORLD OF FRIENDS

GIFTEDNESS AND FRIENDS

Directions: Circle your answer for each question.

1. It's OK if I insist on playing the games I like to play. My friends really don't mind.

   TRUE   FALSE

2. My friends like it when I tell the truth, even when it hurts.

   TRUE   FALSE

3. There is nothing I can do about my crazy emotions or those of my friends.

   TRUE   FALSE

4. To fit in, I have to hide some of my giftedness.

   TRUE   FALSE

5. Being smart and emotional the way I am isn't really *normal*.

   TRUE   FALSE

Chapter 7

TOO MANY CHIEFS

> *"I am really bad at listening to some of my friends. I always feel like I am right—so it's hard to give other kids a chance to speak."*
> —Nina, age 11

Friendships are some of the hardest things for gifted kids to learn to navigate. This is particularly true in school settings, where you often have to learn to work in collaborative groups, sharing responsibilities.

Why are these kinds of settings difficult to manage in the first place? Most gifted kids are natural leaders who believe that their way is the only way to accomplish the task at hand. Like many things with giftedness, the truth isn't so easy. Although you may often know the rules to games better than your peers or know how to spot solutions to problems more efficiently than your classmates and friends, that doesn't mean that you are the *only* one who can figure this out. The trick is learning how to share leadership roles, bend a little on your ideas, and be willing to let your friends have their say in the activity.

SUCCESS SECRET #52

Go easy on your friends.

As a gifted kid, you probably can be very hard on yourself, demanding perfection in everything you attempt. This isn't limited to how you treat yourself. You can be equally demanding of your friends, expecting them to hold themselves to the same level of perfection. Although some of your gifted friends may do this, most of your other friends do not. In fact, most people in the world do not hold themselves to that rigid of a standard. They make mistakes, assume things that aren't true, and don't always remember to think of others.

In short, they are human. And, so are you.

Jumping all over your friends when they make mistakes or accidentally hurt you often makes the situation worse. No one likes to have all of his flaws pointed out. I know you don't. So, don't do that to your friends. Go easy on them, and remember—not everyone can do the things you can. It isn't fair to expect that from them.

"Your friends may not always 'get' you—that's OK. Give them a break, they are trying their best."—Marlene, age 12

SUCCESS SECRET #53 You don't always have to be right.

Shocking, I know. Just like no one expects you to get straight A's on everything, no one really expects you to be right all of the time. In fact, being wrong occasionally, or even just letting someone else be right, is another thing that makes you smart. It means you are willing to take chances. It also means that you are willing to allow someone else to answer questions in class and be the center of attention.

More than anything, it shows the world that you don't need to be *right* in order to have value. By allowing others to experience the joy of getting a correct answer or giving yourself permission to *not* correct someone when you know he is wrong, you are saying that you don't need the approval of others to feel OK. You're saying that it is enough to just be . . . you.

And, you know what? It is!

So, humble yourself from time to time and remember that there will always be someone smarter, faster, and better than you. However, it doesn't matter— because those things do not define who you are on the inside.

"Don't be a know-it-all with your friends. They are probably just as smart as you are."—Roberto, age 13

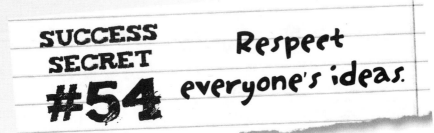

SUCCESS SECRET #54

Respect everyone's ideas.

You like being listened to, don't you? You like having your teacher or parents tell you that you've done something good, right? So do your friends.

It is important as you learn to cultivate friends that you remember that everyone has a need to feel heard and respected. It's part of being a human being. So, how can you show your friends that you respect them?

Allowing them to say what they think is a good start. Others things, like allowing them to be right, letting them pick a game or activity now and then, and treating them with kindness, are all ways you can show respect to your friends.

By doing this, you are saying to a friend, "I appreciate who you are as a person." It also conveys the message that the person has an important place in your life and that you value him. Mutual respect is the key to any true friendship. Without it, there is no trust. And without trust, the foundation for the friendship will crumble.

Take the short quiz below to test your respect know-how.

QUIZ: ARE THESE SIGNS OF RESPECT?

Directions: Circle your answer for each question.

1. Your friend has just given a presentation in class in which you noticed a lot of mistakes regarding the information he presented. Do you:

   a. Point out the mistakes during the presentation?

   b. Talk to your friend afterward and point out the mistakes?

c. Let the teacher handle it? (It really isn't your place to correct your classmate, even if he is your friend.)

2. Your friend is having a hard day and is crying. Do you:
   a. Ignore her completely and walk away?
   b. Ask her what's wrong and insist on helping her settle down?
   c. Ask her what's wrong, but step away if she asks you to give her some space?

3. Your friend just got a new outfit and wore it to school. You don't really think it looks very nice on her. Do you:
   a. Tell her it's hideous?
   b. Tell her you don't like it, but it looks OK on her?
   c. Don't say anything unless she asks, and then ask her if she likes it?

4. Your friend is upset because a classmate just teased him at lunch. Do you:
   a. Tell him to get over it, it's really no big deal?
   b. Tell him to just get the kid back later?
   c. Listen to what he says and try to help him feel better?

If you mostly answered with A's, you have a lot of work to do on recognizing what is and is not respectful. Mostly B's means you are learning, but not quite there. Mostly C's means you are great at respecting other people.

Retake this quiz from time to time to check your respect knowhow and make sure you are on the right track.

SUCCESS SECRET #55

No one likes having her flaws pointed out.

Yes, you do know and see a lot more than the average person. You notice inconsistencies and errors in the world around you. You definitely notice when a friend tells a story wrong, or a teacher misspells a word, or your mom tells your dad something different from what she told a friend on the phone.

You notice it all.

Noticing everything does not mean you should point it all out.

> *"I used to tell people when they were making mistakes on things. I stopped when my friends started getting really mad."—Cassidy, age 9*

As we have said before, people are flawed. That's just the way it is. They make mistakes, they say the wrong things, and sometimes they even lie. Most of the time they don't mean to do these things, it just happens.

And, you know what?

It happens to you as well. There are times when you make mistakes, right? You say the wrong things sometimes, don't you? And maybe, you even tell the occasional lie.

If someone was around to constantly point out these things, do you think you would feel better or worse about things? Yep, that's right—you'd feel worse. Guess what? That's probably how your friends are feeling every time their flaws are pointed out to them.

Think about this before you point out a mistake. Ask yourself if it will help your friend or hurt him. Ask yourself if it is information he needs. Sometimes you will decide that it is. Most of the time you'll realize that pointing out his mistakes is not as important as you thought.

SUCCESS SECRET #56

Give other people a chance to be in charge.

You are a natural-born leader. You take charge of situations easily and have one of those personalities that just likes being the center of attention.

Most of the time, this is a good thing. Your teachers know they can put you in charge and the group will do well. Your friends know this too. They like it when you're in charge; they like getting projects done quickly or how you can pick a game with little effort.

That is, most of the time!

Sometimes your friends may want to be in charge. They may want a chance to organize a project. Or pick a game. Or be first in line.

They may want—or need—to be the center of attention.

Be sensitive to this. Allow your friends a chance to shine. They deserve it as much as you do.

"My dad says I need to let other people be the leader. But, it is really hard to let them. I get frustrated."— Amani, age 8

SUCCESS SECRET #57 Let your friends choose an activity now and then.

Have you ever dreaded going to a friend's house because you knew the same friends would argue about the same things the whole time—who gets to pick what you're going to do, who gets to go first, and what the rules are? You know it happens, probably more often than you'd like to admit. You may even be the one starting a lot of the arguments.

> *"Some of my friends want everything to be done their way—the games we play, the things we talk about. It drives me nuts."—Caleb, age 12*

As we talked about in the previous tip, it is important to let your friends be the leader every now and then. It is also important to let your friends decide what you guys are going to do —the activity, the rules, everything.

I know it's hard to let go of control sometimes. Especially if your friends choose something you don't want to do. If you are going to keep your friends, however, then you need to learn to compromise. That means you need to be willing to do what *they* want to do some days. Trust me, if you all take turns picking activities, all of you will be happier and your friendships will grow stronger.

SUCCESS SECRET #58

Be a problem solver, not a problem maker.

Problems are going to happen in a relationship. There is no way around it. And, problems are not a bad thing. They are really just opportunities to learn new things about your friendship and a chance for the friendship to grow and become stronger.

How you work to solve the problem is important, however. This can often determine if the friendship is going to last or if it is going to end.

There are two ways to approach most problems in a relationship: (1) you can focus on blame, who is right and who is wrong; or (2) you can focus on solving the problems. Usually, you can't do both.

Focusing on blame means all you care about is deciding who caused the problem. It doesn't get you closer to solving it. It doesn't really make you feel better over the long run. It doesn't make your relationship stronger.

Focusing on solving problems, however, does give you and your friend a chance to build a stronger friendship. When you focus on solving the problem, you have to be willing to talk to each other, listen to each other and compromise when coming up with a solution. Problem solving requires both people to be willing to be a little wrong in order to move forward. It also requires shifting the focus away from that and being more concerned with coming up with a way to mend the relationship. Most of the time this means you have to be willing to let go of the things that hurt you and figure out how to not hurt each other in the future.

Being a problem solver means you are willing to see the situation from a different point of view. This can be really hard too. But, being willing to shift how you view things and trying to understand your friend's perspective is a great way to find solutions to almost any problem.

It's like a kaleidoscope; sometimes you need to turn things around to see another solution.

QUIZ: HOW DO YOU SOLVE PROBLEMS?

Directions: Circle your answer for each question.

1. When my friend and I disagree on something, I try my hardest to convince her why I am right.

   TRUE   FALSE

2. When my friend says something mean, I immediately decide she isn't my friend anymore.

   TRUE   FALSE

3. My friends overreact to things all of the time. When this happens, it's better to point out their mistakes and hope they don't do it again.

   TRUE   FALSE

4. Some problems just can't be solved.

   TRUE   FALSE

5. Compromise means my friend will think I'm wrong again.

   TRUE   FALSE

If you answered false to these questions, you are well on your way to becoming a great problem solver. Keep focusing on problem solving and avoid the blame game—these things will help you maintain your friendships.

SUCCESS SECRET #59

Your needs are not more or less important than your friends' needs.

We live in a big world with a lot of people. Recognizing that everyone has needs can be difficult—especially if what someone else needs is different than what you need. Let me ask you something: How can your needs be more important than someone else's?

"My family is really into respecting everyone. But, I get frustrated when others are not respecting people."—Lisa, age 12

The answer is that they can't. Not really.

Everyone's needs are equally important. The trick is to figure out how to get your needs met without hurting someone else.

Needs are not to be confused with wants. You may *want* to be first in line at the amusement park. But, this is not a need—you are probably not going to suffer a terrible fate if you aren't first. If, however, you can't wait in line because of a medical condition, then this want may become a need. In this scenario, standing in line for too long may be an impossible thing for you, and for this reason you may get to go to the front of the line. If someone got mad because you went to the front of the line in this scenario, then that would be wrong. You have a need, and the other person's want should not surpass your need.

Figuring out how to balance your needs with the needs of others requires that you first learn the difference between a need and a want. After that, it takes a lot of practice. It's hard to give up the things you want sometimes. Once you learn to tell the difference between needs and wants, you will quickly learn that you can get your needs met and still respect the needs of others. It isn't nearly as hard as you originally thought.

Parents Sound Off

Your parents know you struggle with friends at times. They recognize your many leadership skills and know too well how hard it is to balance that leadership with strong friendship skills.

» "(My son) hates to waste time. If a project gets stuck over tiny details that delay the group project, he jumps in to guide. That can be a problem for some with the 'I'm the boss' attitude."—Kathleen

» "My daughter hates being around kids that she considers immature. They really seem to annoy her, and she just has no patience for them."—Kellie

» "My son has to be in charge all the time. When he isn't, he complains about everything his friends are doing until they finally let him call the shots again."—Jeff

» "I actually worry about my daughter regarding friendships. She seems to have such a hard time fitting in. Either she is too bossy, or she goes to the other extreme and lets her friends walk all over her. There isn't any in between."—Scott

Take a moment to talk with your parents about friendships. What do they think are your biggest strengths, and what are your areas of difficulty?

Overall, being a good friend means learning to compromise. The tips in this section will help you become better at compromising without sacrificing your needs. Go through the section anytime you feel like you are struggling with your friendships.

What Do You Think?

Take a minute to ask yourself the questions on the next page. The answers will help you as you learn how to be a good friend.

**HOW DO I SHOW RESPECT
TO MY FRIENDS?**

**IN WHAT WAYS DO I CREATE
PROBLEMS? IN WHAT WAYS
DO I SOLVE PROBLEMS?**

**CAN I TELL THE DIFFERENCE
BETWEEN THINGS I WANT AND
THINGS I NEED? CAN MY FRIENDS?**

Chapter 8

> "Never think that because you're smart, you are a nerd. You are whoever you want to be."—Katie, age 12

Every person needs to feel like she belongs—like she has friends that *get* her. For some of you, this is hard to find. Surrounded by people who are interested in different things than you, you may feel like you will never fit in.

Some of you may try to hide your giftedness or blend into the crowd in the hopes that no one figures out how different you are. Others of you may feel like you constantly have to prove your giftedness—to your teachers, your friends, and even yourselves.

The truth is that the easiest way to find good friends or people who will support you no matter what is to be yourself. But, being yourself can be difficult, especially if you aren't sure what that even means.

The next success tips all focus on figuring out who you are and being comfortable with yourself and your friendship choices.

SUCCESS SECRET #60 You have nothing to prove to anyone.

Growing up can be hard. Really hard. This is particularly true when you feel like you have to constantly prove your gifts to everyone. Maybe you struggle in school, despite your giftedness. Or maybe you are in a class with people even brighter than you, so you feel like you can't measure up. Whatever the case may be, sometimes you get stuck feeling like you have to prove your giftedness.

"You shouldn't have to 'prove' your giftedness to your friends or teachers."—Christina, age 11

The truth is that you don't have to prove who you are to anyone. You just have to *be* who you are. Stop trying to blend in, and stop worrying what everyone else is thinking. Go back to the Hula Hoop story and remember that the only thing you have any control over is you and your thoughts and actions. You don't have control over what people choose to think about you, so stop stressing over it.

SUCCESS SECRET #61

Be true to yourself.

Once you stop stressing over trying to prove your giftedness, you can focus on being true to you. How do you do this? The first step is to figure out all of the wonderful things that are true about you, as well as all of the wonderful things that sometimes get in your way. Figure out what it means to be you.

Sometimes you will like what you discover about yourself, and sometimes you will not. Remember that you can change how you react to things and even what you think about them, but you won't be able to change everything. How your body is built is largely due to biology that you can't change. The same is true with skin and eye color, medical conditions, and your giftedness.

Embrace everything about you, and you know what? Other people will too.

"Never stop trying because you want to fit in with 'normal' kids."—Madison, age 11

SUCCESS SECRET #62 — Never try to hide your giftedness—it won't work.

I want to share a little story with you about a girl I once knew. We'll call her Allison. Allison had a very hard time making friends at school. She was a very smart girl, and not at all interested in the things other third graders cared about. Her classmates wanted to play with

> *"My goal this year is to embrace my gifts instead of trying to keep them on the down low."—Savana, age 14*

dolls, but Allison liked to play with chemistry sets. Her classmates liked to read fairy tales, but Allison read Shakespeare. And, her classmates liked to dress up as princesses, but Allison liked to dress up as a doctor.

Allison did not fit in.

One day, Allison decided she would change and be more like her classmates. She stopped playing with chemistry sets, stopped reading Shakespeare, and stopped pretending to be a doctor. She tried to embrace everything her classmates liked to do.

What do you think happened? Did Allison make friends? Was she happy?

You're right . . . she was miserable. And while her classmates did accept her for a little while, Allison could not keep up the charade. Pretty soon she went back to her chemistry sets and Shakespeare. Allison learned that she couldn't change who she was on the inside to please other people. She could only figure out how to be herself.

The good news is that Allison eventually found other kids who understood her unique qualities.

Have you figured out how to embrace your many gifts? Or are you still hiding your giftedness just a little?

SUCCESS SECRET #63

Embrace your friends' intensity.

Making and keeping friends takes more than just finding people who understand you and being true to yourself. It also takes understanding them and their intense feelings.

Just like you, many of your friends are no doubt intense—both in terms of how they think and in terms of how they feel. In order to be a good friend to them, you must learn to embrace their giftedness and their intensities just as you accept your own.

This can be a unique challenge, especially if you are not really comfortable with your own gifted nature. Sometimes, a friend's behavior acts as a mirror, reflecting your own behavior back to you. That can make you feel mad, ashamed, or guilty. You may take these feelings out on your friend, not realizing that you aren't mad at him, you're just embarrassed by your own behavior.

Next time, instead of becoming frustrated by your friend's intense behaviors, embrace them. Show him how much you understand the difficulties of being gifted and support him. Odds are your friend will return the favor one day.

One of the easiest ways to embrace a friend's intensity is to focus on the cool things about your friend and not his behavior. The Making Friendship Cards activity can help you do this.

MAKING FRIENDSHIP CARDS: THE COOL THINGS ABOUT MY FRIENDS

1. On a blank sheet of paper or an index card, list all of the cool things about one of your friends, including the things he does and ways he acts that you really like. Try to remember all of the ways he has been a good friend to you.

2. On the back of the page, make a list of the things that you can do to help your friend feel better when he is having a bad day. Try to come up with at least three things.

3. Make a separate list for each of your friends. (This is where index cards work really well!)

4. Decorate your lists with things that remind you of your friends. Really focus on the things that make them unique. If your friend is into swimming, draw pictures about swimming. If he likes reading, draw pictures of books.

5. Keep your list in a safe place. When a friend's behavior gets a little too intense, pull out your list and remember all of the reasons why you are friends in the first place. Then turn it over and remind yourself how you can help him bounce back and relax.

SUCCESS SECRET #64

Try to understand your friends.

Making a friendship list is a great way to remember the nice things that brought you and your friend together in the first place. Working to really understand your friend can help keep your friendship strong and healthy. But, understanding your friend can be really hard. It requires you to see things from her point of view—something everyone struggles with, even adults.

> "If I want people to understand me, I need to try to understand them."— Emma, age 9

Seeing the world through your friend's eyes means that you try to see why your friend does what she does. It means taking the time to figure her out, and not assuming anything.

I find that the easiest way to know why people do the things they do is to ask them. So, if your friend does something that hurts you, ask her about it. Try not to assume she is mad or upset. In fact, try not to assume anything about her behavior. Instead, ask her about it. Let her tell you why she did or said whatever she did or said.

Trust me, if you take the time to understand her before you react, you will avoid many of the misunderstandings that usually happen in friendships. Your behavior will also encourage her to take the time to understand you as well.

Now, I'm not saying it's easy to stop and try to understand someone, especially if he has hurt you. However, it is the best way to solve problems and maintain friendships. Not to mention, it's just kind. Remember, everyone wants to be understood.

SUCCESS SECRET #65

Look for common interests.

One of the hardest things for gifted kids is finding people with common interests. You are likely trying to fit in with a particular crowd instead of finding people who are interested in the same things you are.

Where can you find people who like the things you do? I would start with clubs or groups at school. Then move into the other areas where you spend a lot of time: church, Scouts, sports, or other activities. Take a chance and try to forge friendships with some of the kids you meet as you participate in different groups. You may not find friends in every setting, but one thing is certain: If you don't try, you won't find any new friends. Besides, you already have one thing in common, right?

FINDING NEW FRIENDS

1. List all of the activities you are involved in during the week.

	Activities	Friends
School		
Church		
Sports		

2. List at least three people you are friends with or would like to be friends with in each area. If you can't think of three, try to think of one.

3. Talk with your parents about your list. Try to arrange a time to hang out with your friends.

4. After you get to know your friend(s) a little, make a list of the things you like to do. Have your friend make a list too. Trade the lists. Do you have some things in common? Are there any things that your friend does that you want to try? This is a great way to broaden your own interests too.

5. Repeat this exercise every now and then. It is a great way to get to know each other and discover new things the two of you can do or learn.

SUCCESS SECRET #66

Find friends who "get" you.

Every person needs a great circle of friends who support him. By learning to understand your friends and looking for common interests, you are well on your way to finding your own mini support group—people who will have your back no matter how hard things get.

A supportive network of friends can help you get through anything that comes your way. They will be the shoulder to cry on when you receive a bad grade, your study group that supports you on that really hard project, the cheerleaders to root for you as you try something new, and the source of comfort you need when things go wrong.

"It's important to have friends that have your back. If you don't, you may want to consider finding new friends."—Tereza, age 13

113

A supportive group of friends doesn't have to mean a large group. For some of you, one or two good friends are all you need. The number isn't important at all—it's the quality of friendship, not the quantity.

It's important as you find your core group of friends to remember that people change over time. Interests change, as do goals. You may find that the things that pulled you and your friend together in third grade no longer apply in fifth. You may find yourself drifting apart. Don't let this scare you. It is normal for friendships to come and go throughout our lifetime. Enjoy your friendships for what they are and the support they give. If you drift apart, don't panic. Some friends are meant to last a lifetime, and some serve a specific purpose in our lives before drifting away. We need both. The important thing is to find people who understand you and to work to keep the relationship strong.

SUCCESS SECRET #67 — Don't take yourself too seriously.

Sometimes friendships end prematurely—not because people move or interests change. Sometimes they end for much simpler reasons: You were too hard on yourself and your friendships, you wanted your friends to make you feel OK, or you expected too much from everyone.

Or you forgot to have a little fun.

> "I wish I knew how to take it easy on myself and my friends when I was younger. It would've helped things—a lot."—Rosi, age 13

Gifted kids naturally take things a little too seriously. Being a deep thinker means that your mind is constantly working and seeing the bigger, harder things in life. Many times you expect big things from yourself, your family, and your friends. There is little room for error.

Relationships aren't like math problems in school: There are seldom single answers to things. People are messy and complicated. There is a way to deal with relationships better. First, stop taking yourself too seriously. Remember that people are flawed, like we discussed earlier. Lighten up—on yourself and your friends. Allow people to make mistakes. Allow yourself to do the same.

And, laugh. Find the humor in life. It will smooth things out.

The more you can remember to relax and allow people to be exactly who they are on any given day, the easier it is to see and appreciate the amazing things they do.

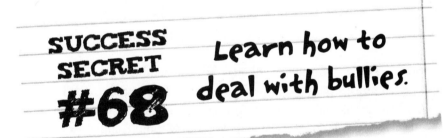

SUCCESS SECRET #68 *Learn how to deal with bullies.*

I could write a whole book about bullies and how to deal with them. As a gifted kid, you may know more than most about being a target for bullying in all of its many forms. Maybe you have even been a bully before. Either way, bullies are no doubt part of your world.

So, what is the best way to deal with bullying? First, it is important to understand what bullying is, and what it is not. There are three questions law enforcement officers use when determining an act of bullying:

» Does the bully have some sort of power over the victim?
» Has some form of aggression—physical or emotional—occurred?
» Does the victim believe the acts of aggression will continue?

If you can answer yes to these questions, odds are good that you have experienced an act of bullying.

There are three typical ways in which someone bullies another person: physical, verbal, and relational (Coloroso, 2009). Let's take a brief look at each of these:

» **Physical**: This is what most people think of with bullies. It is almost always recognized at school and includes hitting, shoving, destroying property, and other acts of physical aggression.

» **Verbal**: This is the most common type of bullying and is usually the way a problem starts. It is easy to get away with, as many teachers and school personnel consider it normal childhood teasing. Verbal bullying includes taunting, gossiping, name-calling, and cyberbullying. This form of bullying, if not dealt with, often leads to physical and relational bullying.

» **Relational**: This is the hardest form of bullying to detect and, in many ways, the most damaging. This type of bullying attacks relationships. It is most often seen in girls and includes deliberately excluding and shunning or ignoring the victim. Like the other forms of bullying, it works to eat away at the victim's feeling about him- or herself.

So, what can you do about bullying? First, remember that no one has the power to diminish you without your permission. Part of the reason bullying, especially relational bullying, works is because you feel powerless to do anything about it. You are left feeling hopeless and without friends—something no one ever wants to feel.

The good news is that you can do something about it. You can choose not to let the behavior of the bully destroy you. You can also report the bully. This is true for you if you are the victim and if you are a witness. Bullies continue to bully because most kids are afraid to do anything about it. You may feel the same way. You may be afraid to get involved, afraid to become the victim, or afraid to be seen as a tattletale.

The truth is that you must report bullies. To do otherwise is to say that their behavior is OK, and we both know it is not.

Learn what it means to bully. Make sure you do not hurt someone else in that way, and if you see acts of bullying, or if you are bullied, know who you can talk to and how you can help. By taking control, you can stop the impact of bullies.

TIPS FOR REPORTING A BULLY

1. Remember what a bully is and is not. Sometimes, especially when you are young, teasing does feel like bullying. Ask your parents and teachers for help if you are unsure.
2. Find out if your school has an anonymous way to report bullying. If it does, use it.
3. If there is no way to anonymously report a bully, talk to your parents about a way to tell the administration about the problem. You may not want to do this, but it really is the only way to make things better.
4. If you are the victim of bullying, use the Hula Hoop technique, your parents, and your friends to work past the bad feelings you may have. Although you can't control what other people do to you, you can control how you feel about it. It may be difficult, but you can move past the hurt.
5. Don't bully others as a response to the pain and hurt you may be feeling. You may be tempted to do it, especially if you're mad. In fact, more than 80% of kids who bully have been bullied at some point. Don't be one of them. Remember how it feels and decide never to do that to others.

Parents Sound Off

Dealing with relationships, friendship drama, and bullying isn't just hard on you—it is usually difficult for your parents as well. Take a look at what your parents think. You may be surprised.

» "Although we have never had to deal with bullying directly, my daughter really freaks out when she sees someone—anyone—being treated unfairly. She comes home and cries about it."—Rashad

» "We have been really lucky in our house. All of my kids have found great friends who share their interests. They really support each other. It's fun to watch them all interact."—LynnAnne

» "I think she struggles with how to deal with her peers sometimes. Maturity is really important to her, and so often kids her age are just complete dolts. She's annoyed by them."—Chara

» "My son had a hard time being accepted as a child. He looked different from the majority of the kids at the school, talked differently, and had different interests. I remember him crying a lot about not fitting in. It was a hard time."—Andrea

Talk with your parents about your friends. Talk with them if you have experienced bullying in any form. They want to know what you think, and you need to know their thoughts too.

Being a good friend means being tolerant of the things about your friend that sometimes annoy you. It also means that your friend tolerates your more difficult qualities too. By learning to appreciate each other, as well as appreciating yourself, you are setting yourself up to have great friendships throughout your lifetime.

What Do You Think?

Time to do a little thinking about friends, being yourself, and bullies. Answer these questions periodically to stay in touch with your ever-changing opinions and friendships.

HOW COMFORTABLE ARE YOU WITH YOURSELF? DO YOU KNOW WHAT YOUR STRENGTHS AND WEAKNESSES ARE? HOW DO YOU DEAL WITH THEM?

WHAT ABOUT YOUR FRIENDS? DO YOU KNOW THEIR STRENGTHS AND WEAKNESSES? HOW DO YOU DEAL WITH THEM?

HAVE YOU EVER BEEN BULLIED OR WITNESSED AN ACT OF BULLYING? WHAT DID YOU DO? WHAT WOULD YOU DO NOW?

Chapter 9

> *"There really is no such thing as normal."*—
> Kane, age 12

Part of developing strong social skills and learning to appreciate others is learning how to appreciate yourself. When you stop trying to be someone different and stop trying to make other people into something different—that's when you begin to find comfort socially, that's when you are strong.

SUCCESS SECRET #69 Accept yourself as you are.

You are an amazing person. You are intelligent and have an almost innate need to learn. You love to throw yourself into the most difficult of projects, but you misspell the simplest of words in your essays. You are both serious and concerned about the world, yet you also find the time to laugh and have fun. You can move from happy to sad so fast it throws you off balance. And, you care deeply about everything.

It can be hard to accept all of these aspects of yourself at times. You may find yourself focusing on the parts of you that you struggle with, things like rigid thinking, or your constant doubt about your giftedness. You may have a hard time seeing your natural intensities as a good thing.

Accepting yourself, however, means recognizing those parts you don't like as well. It means looking for positive ways to think about your difficulties. For example, your rigid thinking can be turned into perseverance, your doubts can be turned into self-reflection, and your intensity can be turned into passion. All of these are admirable qualities. Although you may struggle with how you deal with some of these things, the qualities themselves are a great part of who you are.

MY STRENGTHS

1. List at least three things you consider strengths. Your list could include things like "I do my chores without being asked" or "When I make a promise, I keep it." Be sure to include things that relate to school, friends, and family.

_____

_____

_____

2. List at least three things about yourself that frustrate you. It could be things like "I take too long to do homework" or "I sometimes yell at my friends."

_____

_____

_____

3. Look at your list from Step #2. Can you turn any of those things into a positive quality? For example, with "I take too long to do my homework," can you rephrase that to be a strength? ("I am persistent with my work and strive for my best.")

4. Remember that most of our weaknesses are strengths that we aren't managing well. Focus on the positive.

5. Brainstorm ways to improve the weaknesses you feel you have. If you take too long on your homework, look at the positive attributes of that and then figure out how to manage it better. For example, you know that taking a long time is positive in that it shows your persistence. Manage it better by learning to let go of some things or using tools like a timer to help you stay on track.

6. Read your list of positive attributes every time you find yourself getting down about you.

Rewrite this list often, as your opinions about your strengths and weaknesses will change over time. The important thing to remember is that within every weakness is a strength we aren't really recognizing.

SUCCESS SECRET #70 Accept others as they are.

Once you've figured out how to accept yourself as you are, you need to find a way to accept others as well. This can be tricky. You will often see others' potential, getting more and more frustrated when they don't live up it.

Sometimes you will see the negative things your friends do as personality flaws, instead of viewing them as behaviors that can change. You may forget that we are all just works in progress, changing and developing over time.

Accepting others is necessary for you to develop both empathy (the ability to feel what someone else is feeling) and compassion (the desire to help someone when he is hurting). Building empathy and compassion will help you build your emotional intelligence.

So, first accept yourself—flaws and all. Then, accept your friends. The empathy and compassion you develop along the way will help you in ways you may not realize until you are much older.

TIPS FOR LEARNING TO ACCEPT OTHERS

1. Think about a person you struggle with—someone who really drives you nuts.
2. Focus on the behavior that bothers you, not the person.
3. Write down the things about the *behavior* that frustrate you.
4. Try to see things through the other person's point of view. Can you understand why he behaves the way he does?
5. Try not to judge the other person's behavior. If you are frustrated and can't get past it, talk with him. See if you can work it out. If not, let it go. And remember, it is the behavior that annoys you, not the person.

Accepting others, flaws and all, is something that takes some work to master. As you learn this skill, you will find that accepting yourself will also become easier.

SUCCESS SECRET #71

Don't succumb to the labels.

Sometimes we have a hard time accepting ourselves and others because of the way we have labeled things. You may think you can't like the cheerleader in your class because she is not supposed to be smart or accepting of the smart kids. Or maybe you think that being gifted means you are a nerd, something you are avoiding, so you refuse to think of yourself as gifted because you refuse to believe you are a nerd.

Labels don't really define people, and stereotypes are just that . . . stereotypes. People are often characterized in a certain way because of a certain label, without any regard for who they may actually be.

Labels are around to serve one purpose and one purpose only. They help provide an umbrella of meaning for a specific set of things or people. For example, we label the things we put food on as dishes. Some dishes are made of plastic, some of paper, and still others of clay. They come in a variety of shapes, sizes, and colors, and they serve a variety of purposes. But, we still call all of them dishes.

If we were to assume that dishes only meant a specific type, or size, or shape of dish, we would be wrong—we would be accepting a stereotype.

The same is true about the labels we give to each other. Knowing that you are gifted serves the purpose of telling you about certain ways you may be behaving. Assuming that because you are gifted you must be a nerd, you'll only have a few friends, or you're always right would be wrong. You may or may not like the same things as other gifted people in your class.

"Never think that because you're smart, you are a nerd. You are whoever you want to be."—Kyle, age 9

Never succumb to labels and stereotypes. Instead, take time to figure out who you are on the inside, and do the same with your friends.

SUCCESS SECRET #72 Step out of your comfort zone.

One of the best ways to resist stereotypes and labels is to step out of your comfort zone and broaden your experiences. If you like to read adventure books, try reading fantasy. If you like to play group sports like baseball, try a different type of sport like mountain biking. You don't have to like everything you try—that isn't the point. The point is to broaden your experiences in the world and try new things.

I'm going to challenge you a bit now: I want you to try one new thing every week for a month. It could be a trying a food you never thought you'd like or maybe reading a book that is different for you. It doesn't matter what it is you're trying, it only matters that you do something new each and every week.

After a month or so, write down all of the new things you tried. How did you like them? Which ones would you want to try again?

Repeat this process a few times each year. Before you know it, you will have tried more new things than you ever thought possible.

NEW THINGS I'D LIKE TO TRY

1. List all of the things you would like to try one day. Be crazy when making this list! Don't worry if it isn't realistic.

_____

_____

_____

2. Go through the list and separate your ideas into the following categories:

   a. Things you can try within the next month:

   _____

   _____

   _____

   b. Things you can try in a year or so:

   _____

   _____

   _____

   c. Things you can try as an adult:

   _____

   _____

   _____

3. Focus on the things you can try within the next month or so. What would it take for you to try these? Do you have the ability to access these things?

   _____

   _____

   _____

4. Make a goal to try something new each week. Keep track of the things you accomplish.

5. Find a way to celebrate the new things you have tried each month. Be sure to update your lists as time goes by.

Trying new things is a great way to keep life interesting, not to mention a great way to discover new things about you.

SUCCESS SECRET #73

Enjoy difference.

Human beings have a need to belong and fit in, and those are good things. Recognizing the ways you are unique and enjoying those things are good as well. It's important to find your own voice as you grow up, to discover your own unique way of viewing the world.

Embracing your unique qualities doesn't mean that you should believe that fitting in and common interests are bad. You shouldn't. However, following someone else's lead all of the time—liking only what she likes and doing only what she does—isn't good either.

Like everything else, the trick lies in balancing the two. Learn what things you have in common and what things make you unique. Learn how you and your friends think alike, and how you think differently.

And most importantly, learn how to think for yourself. Sure, you can ask for other people's opinions. But, make *your* own decisions on things, based on what *you* know to be right. This, too, is part of understanding and embracing your uniqueness.

> *"Being different is not a bad thing. In fact, it's pretty cool."*—Giselle, age 10

SUCCESS SECRET #74

Look for ways to be creative.

One of the easiest ways to find your own unique point of view is through creative endeavors. Stretching your creative muscles and looking for new ways of expressing your creativity opens your mind to new ideas and helps create perspective.

Being creative isn't limited to the arts (such as painting, music, and similar activities). Creativity can be expressed through building tasks, words, or even numbers. The possibilities are endless. All it takes is a willingness to try something new without concern of failure. Imagine what you could create if you weren't worried about failing. Imagine what new things you would discover about the world and yourself.

In the first chapter, I talked about finding ways to be creative every day. Creativity helps to develop your problem-solving skills, teaches you how to change your perspective, and fulfills that deep need you feel to learn. It also helps to keep your intensities in balance, by giving you an outlet of expression for all of your emotions. Try it! My guess is that you'll discover just how important expressing creativity really is.

TIPS FOR BUILDING CREATIVITY

1. Make a "create box":
   a. Get an old box that has a lid.
   b. Fill it with leftover art supplies from other projects (such as paper, pens, glue, beads, and feathers).
   c. Use the box during your down time to make . . . anything. Stretch your mind and see what you can create.
2. Limit your TV and video game time. Use the extra time you have to do something creative.
3. Use your computer for creative fun—try making a movie with pictures or creating a blog on an activity you enjoy doing.
4. Think outside of the box. When you have a new project for school, instead of going to the store for new materials to complete the project, look around the house and come up with new uses for things you already have.
5. Work with your parents to create rainy day activities that will help you harness your own creative skills. The resources section at the end of this book is full of links to get you started.

Stretch your creativity know-how in as many areas as possible. By learning to be creative in your approaches to things, you are opening up a whole new way of looking at the world.

SUCCESS SECRET #75

Stay open to new ideas.

As I mentioned in the previous success secret, building your creativity is a great way to learn to see the world from a different angle. By stretching your creative muscles, you allow yourself the freedom of seeing things in a unique way. This, in turn, enables you to understand the different points of view present in any situation. Why does this matter?

Taking a fresh perspective not only helps develop your skills of empathy and compassion (essential pieces of emotional intelligence), but it also helps improve your problem-solving skills and relationships. By being able to see the world from a different point of view, you can begin to understand why people do the things they do or see a new way to solve difficult problems, both those that concern learning and those that concern relationships.

Perspective taking is one of the best ways to learn how to be a good friend. It enables you to clearly see some of the reasons your friends act the way that they do.

TIPS FOR TAKING A FRESH PERSPECTIVE

1. Imagine you are a character in a book. Try to feel what he or she must have felt during one scene of the story.

2. Pick a favorite fairy tale and rewrite the story from a minor character's perspective. For example, rewrite Goldilocks from the point of view of the mother bear or maybe even from the little chair's point of view. How are things different?

3. With a parent's help, stand on top of a chair or the bed. Does the room look different from that view? How?

4. Go with your parents on a drive into the mountains. How do things look different from the peak of the mountains compared to the bottom or the middle? If you don't live near mountains, try imagining this same task from a tall building or monument. For example, does the Lincoln Memorial look different as you move further up the stairs?

5. Draw a picture of your backyard from three points of view:
   a. Sitting in your house and looking outside
   b. Being a bird and flying overhead
   c. Being a small bug and crawling across it

Looking at the world from a fresh perspective is a great way to learn to broaden your views on everything.

SUCCESS SECRET #76 Redefine normal for yourself.

We've talked a lot about normalcy, acceptance, and tolerance over the past few pages. Really, the whole conversation boils down to this: You are the one who needs to define "normal" for yourself.

Yes, your parents, teachers, and friends will influence your ideas. In the end, it is you who will make decisions regarding acceptance. It is you who will decide what is right and what is wrong. You control your thoughts.

> *"Stand up for what you believe in, even if it means you are the only one standing."*—Meghan, age 13

Will you learn to embrace each other's differences and unique qualities? Will you be gentle to yourself and your friends? Will you stand against bullies and take the harder road from time to time?

It takes a strong heart to accept things that are different, and an even stronger heart to defend those in need. In the end, we all live on this planet together—and we all need to find a way to get along.

Parents Sound Off

Parents really understand your unique qualities and how being unique is both a good thing and something you may be struggling with. Check out their thoughts in the quotes below. Any surprises?

» "My two children are in a gifted class at their school. They have told me that they like it a lot because their classmates understand them for the first time. Now, everything they say and do feels normal. I've never seen them so happy."—Bette

» "My daughter struggles to relate to most of her peers. She is not interested in the latest fashions and fads, which makes it hard for her to jump into a conversation with other [kids]"—Tiare

» "My son is a rebel. He really doesn't care what other people think. He does his own thing and seems perfectly happy that way."—Steve

» "My daughter used to struggle making friends, and she couldn't understand why people seemed so mean all of the time. That changed as she got older and began to understand their points of view a bit more."—Judi

Understanding your parents' perspective on you and your unique qualities is a great way to broaden your thoughts. Take some time to talk with them about all of their feelings, and be sure to share your points of view as well.

Learning to embrace your unique qualities and think for yourself can be a challenge at any age, but especially as you enter your preteen and teen years. Review this section as often as you need to in order to remind yourself how to stay true to your own thoughts about yourself and the world.

What Do You Think?

Now it's your turn. Really think about what it means to accept yourself and your friends. Take a few minutes to ask yourself these questions and see how you can develop your empathy and perspective-taking skills.

DO YOU ACCEPT YOURSELF AS YOU ARE? HOW DO YOU SHOW THIS?

DO YOU ACCEPT YOUR FRIENDS AS THEY ARE? HOW DO YOU SHOW THIS?

HOW CAN YOU DEVELOP YOUR CREATIVITY A LITTLE EVERY DAY?

WHAT DOES NORMAL MEAN TO YOU? HAS THE MEANING CHANGED OVER TIME?

Part IV

Parents, siblings . . . nothing can make you feel more loved or bring you more frustration than your family. The burden of parental expectations and the competition you likely feel with your siblings can make things even more complicated as you try to find your footing at home.

This section goes through some of the more common challenges gifted kids may feel at home, covering things like developing good communication skills, learning to set boundaries, and handling mistakes.

But first, let's see what you think about the world of family. Remember to go through this quiz again after you've read this section. Who knows? Maybe your opinions will change!

GIFTEDNESS AND FAMILY

Directions: Circle your answer for each question.

1. Parents have higher expectations for their gifted children.

    TRUE   FALSE

2. I should try to do all of the things I am good at, even if it puts more pressure on me.

    TRUE   FALSE

3. My siblings see me as the competition for our parents' time and attention.

    TRUE   FALSE

4. Having gifted siblings is really hard—competition is inevitable.

    TRUE   FALSE

5. Mistakes at home are a sign that I am not as smart as everyone expects me to be.

    TRUE   FALSE

> *"If your parents offer advice, try to take it. It might help."—Amelia, age 12*

Families can be hard at times—for anyone. Add your normal intensity to the mix, and hard can take on a whole new meaning. You may find yourself struggling to communicate with your parents or siblings. Families are not always easy.

Being a good communicator—knowing what to say and how to say it—is a great way to begin to smooth out any rough spots at home. Learning how to listen, speak without blaming or yelling, and accept advice are all skills that can take you from constant arguments to nice, meaningful chats with your parents and siblings.

SUCCESS SECRET #77 Listening is always more important than speaking.

Did you realize that the words "silent" and "listen" have the same letters? I like to think of it as a reminder that in order to really listen to each other, you must be silent. In that silence you can focus on what your parents or siblings are really saying. You can see the intent of their words through their body language and tone. You can see everything that is unspoken and hear the words that are voiced. But, you can't do this if you're talking or if you're too busy thinking about your next sentence.

"My mom says you have to be quiet in order to listen sometimes. She's right."—Julie, age 13

To effectively listen, you must focus purely on the person speaking.

SUCCESS SECRET #78 You cannot hear if you are yelling.

This secret builds on the last one. Just as you must be silent in order to hear what your parents or siblings are saying, you certainly cannot hear if you are yelling. Think of your last big argument with a family member that resulted in a yell-fest. Did either of you actually hear anything the other person said? Odds are really good you didn't. In fact, as you are remembering it now, you probably don't remember the content of that argument at all.

That's because you were so angry, so focused on getting your point across, that your mind didn't really register the words the other person was saying. The information didn't stay in your mind long enough to wind up in your memory. In addition, because your emotions were running high, you probably couldn't think straight either.

Yelling really accomplishes nothing—it doesn't enable your side of the story to be heard better, it doesn't enable you to hear the other person's side, and it doesn't allow either of you to solve the problem. Really, all it accomplishes is a lot more anger, pain, and maybe even guilt.

I don't know about you, but none of those emotions sound like things I want to feel often.

TIPS FOR OVERCOMING COMMUNICATION PROBLEMS

1. Remain calm. Try to keep your emotions out of the conversation.
2. Clearly state what you want.
3. If you are being asked about something you did, try to answer in a clear and honest way. Try to avoid being defensive and reacting to things.
4. Don't assume that your parents are angry unless they have said that they are angry.
5. Remember, good communication requires good listening skills. Try to listen more than you speak.

Practice these tips often. They really will help improve the communication between you and your family.

SUCCESS SECRET #79

When in doubt, take a break to calm down.

It's normal to feel angry from time to time. No one is better at pushing our anger buttons than our own family. Something about being together day after day and sharing all that is most personal and intimate makes it easier to ignite one another's tempers. Add a little emotional intensity to the equation, and you have the makings for a very explosive situation.

> *"Whenever I get really mad, I have to go into my room for a while and chill. Otherwise I just yell at everyone."—Marie, age 13*

There is a way to control it, however: Take a break before things get out of hand. The key is to recognize that you need a break, and take it before it's too late. We all have a point where all we can do is yell, a point where it is impossible to pull back from the explosion. What you need to do is figure out where your breaking point is and remove yourself from the situation *before* you reach it.

This is often easier said than done. But, if you really utilize this success secret, you will keep yourself from blowing up and develop a habit of managing your anger.

SUCCESS SECRET #80

Don't argue with your parents— it accomplishes nothing.

Parents. They seem to have an answer for everything, and usually it feels like a lecture. When you're young, their words of wisdom are little jewels you collect, using them to help shape how you think and feel about things. This begins to change as you get older.

As the lectures feel more familiar and frequent, they lose some of their appeal. Before long, you feel yourself wanting to disagree or maybe even argue with their words. Don't be alarmed. It happens in every parent-child relationship sooner or later. Don't be silly enough to give into that feeling either.

Arguing with your parents is a lot like arguing with your teacher—it seldom gets you what you want. Yes, there are good reasons for talking with your parents and letting them know what you need or want. It is good to tell them your opinions on things, even if those opinions are different.

Your parents may encourage the debate, asking for your reasons of disagreement. Eventually, though, your parents will come to a decision. The time for discussion or debate will be over. If your parents decide to do something different than what you think is right or fair, you may want to prove your points over and over again, hoping to change their minds. Just because you want to do this, doesn't mean you should. In fact, rehashing your opinions will always seem like arguing and will usually result in problems, sometimes big problems.

Instead, listen to your parents. They may have specific reasons for making the rules and decisions that they make. Give them the benefit of

> "Just remember that your parents just want you to do the best you can. Their intentions are good, even if you don't agree. So hear them out."—Amy, age 14

the doubt that they are working in your best interest, even if it doesn't feel that way to you.

You will still get mad. And, you'll still want to argue. You just need to learn to resist that urge and let things go. Trust me, things will be much smoother at home if you do.

SUCCESS SECRET #81

Be willing to talk about your mistakes.

It is hard to openly discuss the poor choices you make with people, especially with your parents. You may want to deny the mistakes or pretend you didn't make them. Or, you may want to blame your behavior on something else and justify your errors somehow. None of this helps in the long run. In fact, it pretty much guarantees more problems with your parents.

As we have discussed many times throughout this book, every person makes mistakes throughout his lifetime. Some of them are little, some are big, and most are not made intentionally. Mistakes don't define who you are—not by a long shot. What you do with the mistakes, however—how you respond—that is what speaks to your character.

So, the next time your parents want to discuss some of your mistakes, don't assume they are looking to find fault with you. They are really just trying to help you learn from the errors that you make. They are trying to help you grow.

> *"Talk about your mistakes with family and friends. Turn them into lessons that help you improve."*—Akeem, age 13

SUCCESS SECRET #82 Stay calm when discussing hard topics.

Have you ever noticed that parents really want to talk about hard things sometimes? Have you also paid attention to how you react when asked to talk about the hard stuff?

"I've never actually won an argument by getting angry and yelling."—Scott, age 12

Odds are you clam up, refusing to utter more than a few one-word answers to their questions. You may get angry and react to their questions by yelling. Or, you may try to leave the conversation as quickly as possible. Regardless of which reaction is most common for you, the truth is that it's hard to talk about certain things.

What kinds of things are hard to talk about? For some of you it could be grades or problems at school. For some, it could be risky choices you have made. For others, it may involve serious family situations like divorce. All of these topics can result in a conversation that quickly leads to heated tempers and yelling.

So, how do you stay calm when talking about the hard stuff? How do you keep your cool even when your blood is boiling? The answer lies in understanding what kinds of things make you angry to begin with, as well as a plan to stay calm when you are angry.

Remember how you can't think when you're stressed and frustrated? Well, the same thing applies to anger. Your brain doesn't make good decisions when you are angry. Staying calm by taking a break or doing some of the relaxation techniques from the first section of this book are great ways to fight back the anger and stay calm.

Keeping your cool helps you understand whatever it is your parents are saying. It also helps keep the situation from becoming explosive. The next time you find yourself getting angry when your parents start talking about your grades or another hard topic, take a deep breath and calm down. Who knows, you may discover that they only want to give you some advice you can use.

SUCCESS SECRET #83

Avoid blame.

The blame game: We're all guilty of playing it from time to time as we try to justify our behavior in some way. Maybe we say someone else did something we are guilty of doing. Maybe we blame not doing our homework on leaving stuff at school, or we say that the teacher wasn't clear about it when the truth is that we just didn't pay attention. Sometimes the blame game is used to justify problems with friends and issues with our sibling.

No matter how you use blame as a way to justify your poor choices, you need to know that blaming other people or other situations for our own behavior solves nothing.

Most of the time, your parents will know when you are choosing to blame someone or something for your own mistakes. And, most of the time, the consequence for your actions is more severe if you blame others first.

Most kids don't know when they are playing the blame game. You may not always recognize that making excuses for your behavior is a form of the blame game. For example, let's say you forgot your book at school. Saying that you were tired and forgot, or saying that a friend distracted you, are ways of blaming the action (you forgot your book) on something else (fatigue or the friend) instead of owning up to your behavior.

Here's the thing: Blaming others never solves a problem. Blaming others negates the truth of the Hula Hoop rule. You, your thoughts, and your actions are always within your control. Always.

Now, that doesn't mean you won't make mistakes. We've already established that you will. Sometimes you will forget to think a problem through before you act. Or, you won't think about the consequences for your actions.

These are all things that will likely happen at some point. However, saying that you are not to blame because of these things only makes the problem even worse.

You are always in control of you—regardless of whether or not you remember that fact. So, the next time you are asked about something you may have done, do yourself a favor: Take responsibility for your actions and avoid the blame game completely.

TIPS FOR AVOIDING THE BLAME GAME

1. Always accept responsibility for your actions—even if you didn't mean to do whatever you did.
2. Remember the Hula Hoop trick. Don't look for loopholes that get you out of trouble. Just admit your mistakes.
3. Even if you feel out of control at times, you are still responsible for your actions. Avoid the temptation to blame your behavior on these things:
   a. "I'm tired."
   b. "I didn't understand."
   c. "I can't control my tone of voice."

4. Make a list of the things you tend to blame your behavior on. Then make a plan to avoid using those things in the future.
5. Ask your parents to partner with you on this. Develop a word or phrase they can use when they notice that you have fallen into the blame game.

Avoiding the blame game is the quickest way to take control of your own behavior and change it for the better.

SUCCESS SECRET #84 Accept responsibility for your actions.

As soon as you stop blaming others for your actions and as soon as you recognize that you are the only one responsible for the things you do, the sooner you will begin to learn from the mistakes that you make.

Accepting responsibility, as I stated earlier, begins with the recognition that you are the only one calling the shots in your behavior. This can be a difficult thing to accept. Most of us do things to please our teachers or our parents. We don't do things only to please ourselves, and that's a good thing. It is important to understand the expectations of others and follow the rules we are given.

That being said, living up to expectations and following rules do not give you an excuse for your behaviors. You do not get to blame what you do on the rules or on a teacher or parent's expectations. Ultimately, it is still up to you to figure things out. You choose your actions, both consciously and unconsciously. You determine the things that you do, whether you meant to or not.

Part of being responsible means accepting that you are in control of your actions—that you always have a choice regarding your behavior.

QUIZ: AM I RESPONSIBLE?

Directions: Circle your answer for each question.

1. When I do something I know is wrong, I own up to my mistake before my teachers or family confront me.

   TRUE   FALSE

2. When my mother asks me about a mistake I have made, I resist the urge to give an excuse for my behavior.

   TRUE   FALSE

3. My friends and teachers know that I will own my behavior, whether I've done a good thing or a not-so-good thing.

   TRUE   FALSE

4. My parents just found out that I received a bad grade on a test. When they confront me I say that I didn't study enough and admit my mistakes.

   TRUE   FALSE

5. I think it is important to own my mistakes in all situations.

   TRUE   FALSE

If you answered true to these questions, you are a pro at accepting responsibility for your actions. Remember that owning your mistakes is the first step toward being responsible and an important part of growing up.

Parents Sound Off

Being the parents of a gifted child can be a hard job. They have to balance what they expect from you with what you need from them. It can be as confusing and frustrating for them as it is for you. Check out their words and see if you discover anything new about the things that some parents feel and say. Then take a moment to find out how your parents feel.

» "My child is (easily) frustrated by adult-imposed boundaries at home and school."—Tara

» "It's hard as a parent—you don't always know when they need help or just a little motivation. Sometimes you need to push but are afraid to push too much. It gets really complicated."—Sherrie

» "My kids think we are always yelling at them. Sure we are firm, but yelling? No. We don't yell."—John

» "Parenting my gifted children has been both my biggest joy and my biggest headache. I love all the neat ways they think. But their emotions do tend to take over the house from time to time."—Donita

Bottom line, it's important to remember that parents want the same things you do—the ability to communicate well with you and help you when you ask.

Communication is a tricky thing, but taking the time to work through these tips will give you the tools you need to resist the common problems that arise between parents and kids as you approach your teen years. These tips will also give you the habits that will make those often turbulent years much smoother.

What Do You Think?

Families can be the biggest source of comfort and pain for anyone. Take a few moments and answer these questions for yourself to see how you feel about communicating with your parents.

WHAT ARE YOUR BIGGEST
ROADBLOCKS TO COMMUNICATION
WITH YOUR PARENTS? WHAT
CAN YOU DO TO REDUCE
THESE ROADBLOCKS?

EVERYONE NEEDS A FEW TRICKS
TO STAY CALM WHEN TALKING
ABOUT HARD THINGS. WHAT
ARE YOUR FAVORITE TRICKS?

HOW DO YOU DEMONSTRATE
THAT YOU HAVE ACCEPTED
RESPONSIBILITY FOR YOUR ACTIONS?
WHAT PART OF BEING RESPONSIBLE
DO YOU STILL STRUGGLE WITH?

Chapter 11

> *"I have a real problem with overscheduling. There are just too many things I want to do. And, of course, I always want to do them per-fectly."—Lizbeth, age 14*

Balancing all of the expec-tations you may feel from school, your friends, parents, and yourselves can be hard. Most gifted kids feel an innate obligation to share their giftedness . . . everywhere. Couple that with a keen interest in many different kinds of activ-ities, and it is easy to see why so many gifted kids find themselves overscheduled.

Learning about setting boundaries and how you spe-cifically renew is crucial if you are going to learn to manage the expectations you feel from others and yourself.

SUCCESS SECRET #85

You don't have to do everything well.

> "I try to do my best, but that doesn't mean I'm going to be perfect." —Robert, age 13

Yep, I'm saying it again—you are not expected to be perfect. This means that no one expects that everything you do will be perfect either. There will be things that are hard for you. Take me, for example. I'm great at figuring out math problems. I am also good at understanding complicated stories. But learning languages? I'm horrible at mastering other languages. I just can't seem to get the hang of it, no matter how hard I try. One of my best friends, on the other hand, has mastered not two, but three other languages. I don't know how she does it!

Now, just because I don't learn languages well doesn't mean I didn't try hard. I did. I studied and studied—I had to. It was the only way I could pass my language classes in college.

At first, I felt sad and frustrated that I couldn't master languages as well as I could everything else. Eventually I realized the truth . . . I wasn't going to be perfect at everything I tried.

It's a hard lesson for most gifted kids to learn, but it can be the most freeing too. By realizing that you don't have to be perfect at everything, you can give yourself permission to try things for fun—not because you *have* to excel at them.

SUCCESS SECRET #86

Just because you can do something, doesn't mean you have to.

Although you aren't expected to do well at everything you try, the truth is that there are a lot of things you will be very good at. You may feel that you want to do them all. What happens if you take on everything that you can excel at doing? You'll get overwhelmed.

You are going to have to learn that you can't commit to doing everything—you need to balance out the things you must do for school, with your other commitments for extracurricular activities, with the things you are expected to do at home. Try hard to keep everything in balance, realizing that talking on too much leads to only one thing . . . stress.

"You need to learn to limit how much you take on. Trust me, I know. Taking on too much leads to stress."—Maggie, age 13

SUCCESS SECRET #87

Set good boundaries.

Part of learning to not take on too many activities at once is learning to set good boundaries for yourself. Setting boundaries relates to understanding your roles at school, with your friends, and at home, as well as understanding how and when to say no to things.

Understanding your roles in the various aspects of your life is an important first step. At school, you take on the role of student. Your job in this role is to do the best you can on your assignments and learn everything the teacher is attempting to teach. It is not your job to make sure everyone else is learning. That is the job of the teacher. Staying clear on this helps you keep from losing out on your own learning because you have been so busy helping your classmates. Now, this doesn't mean you shouldn't help, but helping to the point of neglecting your own needs doesn't show good boundaries.

Your role in friendships is to be a good friend: kind, loyal, and supportive. It is not your role to *parent* your friends—to tell them what and how to think. That doesn't mean you can't share your ideas. You can and you should. But, respecting your role as a friend means you understand the limits of that role.

At home, you are in the role of child. It is not your job to be the parent of the house or to dictate the rules. Although this may happen occasionally, observing good boundaries helps set a solid foundation for all family members.

Another aspect of boundaries involves saying no to some things. This is a very hard thing for most gifted kids and adults to do. With a few tricks, learning when to say no gets easier.

Start by setting goals and clarifying what you are trying to achieve. If your goal is to get straight A's in school, then saying yes to a study party may be a good thing. If, on the other hand, you want to ace your test tomorrow, saying yes to an invitation to go to the mall when you should be studying would work against you.

In addition to setting goals and figuring out what it is you are hoping to achieve, you need to develop a good sense of how you function in terms of stress. All of us have a certain way we act when we are overwhelmed by things. For some, you may withdraw from everyone or get sick. For others, you may feel like you are angry all of the time. The key is figuring out what is true for you. Learn your signs that you have taken on too much and learn what to do to balance yourself back out.

TIPS FOR SETTING REALISTIC BOUNDARIES

1. Begin by listing everything you are involved in and every role you have. Remember to include activities from church, sports, and any other things you are involved in. I have listed a few things to get you started:
   a. Daughter/Son
   b. Student

   c. _____

   d. _____

   e. _____

   f. _____

2. Next to each role, list your responsibilities. For example, next to daughter/son, you may want to list things like following the rules, supporting my parents, and so on.

3. Rearrange the list in order of priorities: Which roles are the most important? List those first.

4. Look over the list. Can you do all of the things you have listed without exhausting yourself? Compare the list to your goals. Do they line up?

5. If you need to cut some things out, start at the bottom. Also, look over the responsibilities you've listed under each role. Are these things that you *must* do? If not, see where you can adjust.

The important thing to remember is that you are not expected to do everything and be everything to everyone. You must learn to separate what is realistic for you to do from what is unreasonable.

SUCCESS SECRET #88

Respect the boundaries of others.

In addition to learning how to set your own boundaries and how to say no, you need to learn how to respect the boundaries of others. This can sometimes be difficult. Gifted kids are naturally adept at convincing other people to adopt their point of view. Sometimes this leads to pushing other people into situations that violate their boundaries.

It is important to learn how to respect other people's boundaries and remember that no really does mean no. It isn't an excuse to practice your strong verbal skills and turn the no into a yes—even if that has worked in the past.

Learning to respect other people's boundaries is a great way to help them respect yours. It also helps you learn how to balance the needs of others with your own needs.

> "It's one thing to try to persuade someone to do what you want, it's another to bully them into doing it."—Enrique, age 14

SUCCESS SECRET #89

Know the household rules and follow them.

Rules, rules, rules. We all have rules we must follow in this world. Some of the rules come from our teachers, and some come from our friends, but most come from home.

Household rules are something we learn at very young age. They may change periodically, but for the most part, they stay the same throughout our childhood. Knowing and following the rules of the house is something every parent expects from you. But, what if you don't agree with some of the rules? Or, you don't really know them? What then?

It is important to know how to talk with your parents if you are confused about the rules themselves or if there is something you would like to change. Here are a few tips for talking to your parents about the rules:

» Be respectful.
» State your concerns clearly and with little emotion.
» Be sure to listen to their response.
» Don't argue.

Following these tips will enable you to have a calm conversation with your parents about the rules and the concerns you have.

MY LIST OF HOUSEHOLD RULES

1. List all of the rules you know about in your household.

   _____

   _____

   _____

2. Ask your parents to review the list with you. Do they agree with the rules you have listed? If not, adjust the list as needed.
3. Look over the list. Are there any rules you are confused about or disagree with? Talk these over with your parents.
4. Are there rules you think need to be added to the list? Discuss these as well.
5. Keep the list someplace where you can refer to it from time to time.

It isn't important what kinds of rules you have at home or even how many. But, it is important that you understand them and know the consequences for following and not following the rules. If any of this is confusing to you, be sure to sit down with your parents and calmly discuss it. It's hard to comply with the rules when you are unclear as to what they are in the first place.

SUCCESS SECRET #90

Balance, balance, balance.

We've talked a lot in this chapter about boundaries and not taking too much on at once. The key is learning to achieve balance.

Easier said than done.

Achieving balance begins with taking good care of yourself. Refer back to Success Secret #15 on taking care of yourself and the tips on pp. 24–25. Make sure that you are doing the things listed, including getting enough sleep and learning to relax.

In addition to practicing the strategies listed in Success Secret #15, it is important to understand how you renew your emotional self. Most people renew in one of two ways: alone or with others. Renewing in solitude, also known as being an introvert, means that you can get cranky when you are around people for too long. It may also mean that you prefer to be alone, reading a good book or putting together a puzzle (Sword, 2006b).

Those of you who renew through social connections, also called extroverts, often need to talk with someone in order to feel rejuvenated. You may need to retell your day just to relax. You may get stressed when you don't have people around you.

Just like you renew in particular ways, so do the people around you. It is important to have some idea as to how they renew—this way you can learn to respect their needs as you seek to get your own met.

QUIZ: HOW DO I RENEW?

Directions: Circle your answer for each question.

1. You come home from a busy day at school and your mom immediately asks you how your day was. Do you:
   a. Cringe and answer as briefly as possible, hoping she'll just be quiet for a little while?
   b. Eagerly tell her all about your day, excited to share?

2. Your teacher assigns a group project at school. Do you:
   a. Ask her if you can do it alone, knowing you hate working with other kids?
   b. Look forward to sharing your ideas with another person, even though you are a little nervous about group projects?

3. It's the first day of school. Do you:
   a. Watch what the others are doing, waiting to understand the class expectations before you participate more actively?
   b. Sit down with the first group of people you see and introduce yourself?

4. You've been invited to a party with several friends. Do you:
   a. See if you can go to the party with a friend, not wanting to show up alone?
   b. Tell your friends you'll meet them there, not caring if you go alone or not?

5. Would you rather:
   a. Read a book?
   b. Play a game with a friend?

If you mostly answered with A's, you are more introverted, needing solitude to renew throughout the day. Mostly B's means you crave the attention of others in order to renew. Some of you may have struggled with answering the questions, feeling that both answers were true. In those cases, go back and pick the answer that is most often true. Most people will find themselves more introverted or more extroverted.

SUCCESS SECRET #91

Don't overcommit.

You did it: You set your goals, you learned about boundaries, and you are busy respecting other people's needs and boundaries. You have figured out how to renew each day and are in the habit of taking good care of yourself. So, how is it that you've still managed to overcommit?

There are going to be times when setting goals isn't enough to ensure that you don't take on too much. At those times you will need to learn to decide between the many important things you have on your plate. You will need to learn to limit what you get involved in.

It won't be fun, and you won't like some of the choices you may have to make. Sooner or later every gifted kid needs to learn how to keep from overcommitting, if for no other reason than to prevent the inevitable emotional explosion that usually happens.

> *"Sometimes you have to choose between friends and family. Family should always come first."—Allison, age 13*

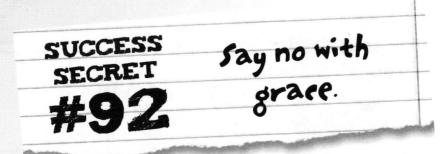

SUCCESS SECRET #92

Say no with grace.

A lot of kids have a hard time saying no when they are asked to do something. You may worry about how the person will react to your answer. You may also worry that he will think less of you because you aren't participating in whatever he is asking you to do. And, sometimes, you just don't say no because you don't know how.

Saying no with grace takes a little practice, especially if you need to say no to something you want to do or feel obligated to do. Begin by remembering why you are saying no in the first place—because you have no time or energy to take on more activities. Thank the person for thinking of you and kindly let him know that your current commitments make it impossible for you to take on another thing. If you remember to be kind and honest, the person will not feel rejected by your no.

> *"I hate saying no when people ask me to do things because I hate feeling like they are going to be mad at me. I guess I just haven't learned how to say it nicely yet."—Danielle, age 10*

Parents Sound Off

Parents know all too well how many things you tend to load on your plate. School, sports, extracurricular activities—the list is often endless. But, unlike you, they don't always see that their expectations are part of the reason you may find yourself so busy. Take a look at their quotes to help gain a fresh perspective on their opinions of the expectations and other things you may struggle to balance.

» "There is no bigger burden than having to carry others' expectations around your whole life."—Kathleen

» I expect my daughter to always try her best, even when something is hard, but on the other hand, not to take herself too seriously."—Tiare

» "Sometimes my daughter would really just like to be like everyone else, without all the expectations. She doesn't see that most of those expectations are because she puts them there."—Nichole

» "Teaching my kids how to say no to things, how to not overburden themselves with activities, has been one of the hardest things we've ever done. I still don't think we managed a very good job with it."—James

Take a moment to talk with your parents about these things. You may find that they expect less than you think.

Finding your balance is a hard thing. So is managing the expectations you feel from everyone, including yourself. Review the tips in this chapter and the questions below often. The better you are at living a balanced life, the more you will be able to accomplish in the long run, and the better you will feel.

What Do You Think?

Setting good boundaries and balancing expectations can be a difficult thing for gifted kids to learn. Think about the success secrets you've read and look at the following questions. Answering them will give you insight regarding your own feelings about expectations and setting good boundaries.

BEING HONEST WITH YOURSELF,
DO YOU THINK YOU SOMETIMES
TAKE ON TOO MUCH? TOO LITTLE?
IS IT A PROBLEM FOR YOU?

WHAT DO YOU NEED TO RENEW
EACH DAY AND STAY IN BALANCE?
WHAT ARE THE BIGGEST
BARRIERS TO ACHIEVING THIS?

IT CAN BE HARD TO MAINTAIN
GOOD BOUNDARIES WITH FRIENDS
AND FAMILY. DO YOU CONSIDER
YOURSELF GOOD AT SETTING
AND MAINTAINING BOUNDARIES,
OR IS THIS SOMETHING
THAT IS HARD FOR YOU?

Chapter 12

> "There's nothing worse than when my mom tries to take over my homework and tell me how to do it. I know what I'm doing and I wish she would trust me to get it done."— Bianca, age 14

Your parents give you advice all of the time. Your teachers are constantly sharing a better way of doing things. Heck, even this book is giving you secrets to success. Everyone seems to be giving you some advice on how to be you, almost as if you aren't enough as you are.

At least, that's how it seems to you.

Advice is not a bad thing. Receiving advice does not mean that the person giving it thinks you are somehow wrong. Usually the advice is given out of kindness, as a way to help you see a different way of doing something. Learning how to give and receive advice is a great way to improve your relationships at home, as well as become a stronger individual.

SUCCESS SECRET #93

Your siblings are part of Team You.

We've talked a lot about family and how it can support you. For some of you, family means more than just your parents. It can mean siblings, grandparents, aunts, uncles, and cousins. Family refers to all of the people in your inner circle. These people know you in ways that are different from friends. They support you and are often your biggest fans—even when you don't do as well as you wanted to.

Sometimes, it's hard to connect with your family. This can be especially true with siblings. Sometimes you may feel competition with them, as if each of you is somehow vying for your parents' love and affection.

The truth is that your siblings will often be your best supporters. Yes, there is a lot of natural competition with your brothers or sisters. In the end, it is usually these same people that provide some of the best support—when you can remember that they are part of your team.

"The best part of having my sisters is how we all 'get' each other. Of course that also means that our disagreements are pure chaos."—Marlene, age 12

SUCCESS SECRET #94
Your parents are your allies.

Just like siblings and extended family member are your cheerleaders, your parents are usually your best allies. They are there to guide you and help you navigate through the difficult journey of growing up. They can be your partners and support group.

"If I can remember that my parents are trying to help, I don't get as mad."—Elena, age 10

Like in any partnership, there are times when you are going to get frustrated with them. Maybe you don't see eye to eye with their rules or their advice. Maybe it feels like they are trying to stop you from growing up at times. And, maybe they are in some ways.

But, your parents are your allies in the long run. Much of the advice they offer and the rules they impose serve a purpose you can't really see or understand when you are young. Appreciate your parents and all of the ways they try to guide you. If their advice doesn't seem to work, talk with them. Ask questions and work together. After all, a healthy partnership is not a one-sided deal.

SUCCESS SECRET #95

Making a mistake is not the end of the world.

One of the more common reasons kids and their parents get into arguments has to do with mistakes. Often a child will break a family rule or make a mistake at school. The parent will then talk with the child to try to determine what happened. Eventually that conversation leads to consequences of some form and a lot of hurt feelings on both sides (especially as you get older and you get better at making your parents feel guilty).

Your parents know that you are going to make mistakes during your childhood—they expect it. And, as we've discussed many times already, you should expect that you will make a few mistakes as well. What gets you into trouble isn't just the mistake, it's the way the mistake is handled.

Did you admit the error or did you fall into the blame game trap we've discussed in earlier chapters? Were you willing to talk about the mistake calmly or did you yell and argue? Did you try to learn from the situation or did you refuse to accept responsibility for your actions? All of these things determine how your parents will react to the mistake made.

No matter how things go, no matter if you react in a way that makes the mistakes worse, it is still not the end of the world. Let me repeat that: Making a mistake is *not* the end of the world. It's only a mistake, a chance to learn something new and try again.

WHAT TO DO IF YOU MAKE A MISTAKE

1. First and foremost, you must admit the mistake.
2. Make apologies or anything else you need to do to demonstrate your ownership of the mistake.
3. Ask yourself *why* you made the mistake. Did you forget something (like writing down an assignment) or did you just not think about the rules? Be as honest as you can on this.
4. Come up with a plan to avoid making the same mistake again. If you forgot something at school, how can you keep yourself from forgetting again?
5. If the mistake caused a second problem, do you need to address that problem also? For example, if forgetting your assignment at school caused you to fail a class, what must you do to address that failure now?

Everyone makes mistakes from time to time. It is important to look at these mistakes not as failures, but as opportunities to learn and grow. What can you learn from the mistake you made?

SUCCESS SECRET #96 Mistakes do not equal stupid.

> "Making mistakes is normal."
> —Erika, age 10

I think the difficulties gifted kids have with making mistakes lies in the incorrect belief that mistakes mean you're not gifted. Nothing is further from the truth: Not when it comes to mistakes on homework, and not when it comes to mistakes that are much bigger.

It is true that sometimes people act without thinking. It is also true that many poor choices happen during those times. Even then, however, although the behavior was less than we may have wanted or expected from ourselves, it does not mean we are stupid. Or bad. Or fatally flawed.

As I said on the success secret above, making a mistake *only* means one thing—that you made a mistake. Trying to make it mean something more only serves to make you more stressed and more afraid of making poor choices.

SUCCESS SECRET #97

Admit your mistakes.

Although making mistakes is a normal part of growing up, it doesn't mean you aren't obligated to deal with the error and the consequences of the error in some way.

As I mentioned earlier, most of the problems that come from poor choices happen as a result of how you chose to deal with your own behavior. Pretending the mistake didn't happen, or worse, lying about it, only makes things worse between you and your parents. It creates an even bigger problem.

There are many reasons you may want to lie or blame someone else for your mistakes. I talked about some of the reasons when I reviewed the blame game—things like avoiding the consequence or avoiding feeling like you failed at something. Most of the time, you just avoid taking ownership for your choices and behaviors because it's hard. You may think that admitting your error makes you a disappointment in the eyes of your parents, teachers, and friends. Maybe you feel like the mistake confirms that you aren't worthy of your parents' trust and love. Or, maybe you're just really afraid of being in trouble.

The truth is that mistakes themselves have no bearing on your worth. As we have already said—what you choose to do with the mistake, how you choose to respond—that demonstrates more about you than the error you've made.

So, now you're convinced that you must admit your mistakes in order to move forward. But, how? Yes, you must take responsibility as we've discussed earlier in this section.

"I really struggle when it comes to admitting my mistakes. I don't know, it just always feels like when I admit a mistake it means I am not gifted, not perfect. I hate feeling like I am not perfect."—Ami Jane, age 12

Sometimes that can be tricky. Gifted kids are very good at fooling people, especially themselves. It would be easy for you to convince yourself that the situation really isn't your fault or that the mistake isn't that bad at all. It's hard to be objective about your own behavior and even harder to tell when you aren't. Hard or not, however, admitting your mistakes is the only way to give yourself an opportunity to learn from them and avoid repeating the same mistakes in the future.

SUCCESS SECRET #98

Make amends for your mistakes.

The next step in dealing with mistakes is making amends. This means not only admitting the problem, which you have already done, but taking steps to deal with the consequences of the error.

Let's say you cheated on a test and got caught. The first thing you have to do is admit that you did it. Then you need to find a way to make amends. In my house, that would entail an apology to the teacher, as the act of cheating is a sign of disrespect. In your house, it could be something different.

What you do to make amends isn't as important as actually doing it. Find a way to make up for the mistake and do it. Talk with your parents and the person you wronged. See how you can fix the problem.

There will be times when you can't fix things. This is particularly true if the error you made resulted in someone else being hurt physically or emotionally. But there is always a way you can make amends, even if it doesn't fix the problem.

TIPS FOR MAKING AMENDS

1. First admit the mistake to the person you wronged.
2. Ask that person if there is a way you can "make things right."
3. If there is a way to make things right, be sure to do it quickly and without complaint.
4. Make a plan to avoid making the same poor choice in the future.
5. Let it go. Don't define yourself and your self-worth by the mistake you have made.

One of the hardest things about mistakes and making amends is the tendency to define yourself by your mistakes. Avoid this trap as much as possible and remember that everyone makes mistakes. Taking the time to make amends for your mistakes is one of the best ways to show your responsibility and willingness to learn.

SUCCESS SECRET #99 Seek reconciliation.

Reconciliation, or finding harmony, is the last step in moving forward after making a big mistake. It follows admitting the problem and making amends and involves seeking forgiveness, typically through an apology.

Although this step may seem simple, forgiveness isn't something you can control. Sure, you can admit what you have done, apologize for your actions, and find a way to make amends. But, doing all of that does not necessarily mean the person you wronged will forgive you. That choice is completely up to them. Just as it is your choice to decide how you will act and feel in a variety of situations, everyone has a similar choice.

There will be times when a mistake isn't forgiven, when something you have done can't be fixed with an apology. In those situations, you have to figure out how to release your own guilt and move forward.

For gifted kids this can be really tough. As with many things, you tend to feel guilt very deeply. As a result, you may struggle to let go of a mistake when someone isn't accepting your apology. You may try over and over to convince the person to forgive you. And, it may not work. At all. That is the other person's choice, just as it was yours to ask for his forgiveness.

"I really have a hard time when a friend can't forgive me. It always makes me feel like I have done some horrible, horrible thing. I need to try to remember that even if someone doesn't forgive you for something you've done, it doesn't mean you can't forgive yourself."—Akira, age 9

If a friend chooses not to forgive you after a mistake, you have to let it go. You have done what is required of you—you accepted your part of the problem. You tried to make amends. And you sought reconciliation. There is nothing else you can do in the situation. So stop twisting yourself into a mess to make him forgive you. Learn to let it go.

SUCCESS SECRET #100

No one is ever really alone.

As a gifted kid, you know what it feels like to be alone at times. You know that not everyone gets you all of the time. You know you think differently than most of the people you know. You know that you are pretty unique. But, this doesn't mean you are alone.

No one is as alone as they feel at times. There are always people around that you can lean on, even if you've never leaned on them before. The problem is, you seldom remember who all of the members of your support team are when you are in the middle of a crisis. As a result, you may feel very lonely even though there are people in your life to help you.

Take a minute to think about all of the people you can turn to when you need support. Think of your family, your friends, and even your teachers. Take a few minutes and complete the worksheet below. It will help you remember that you are not alone.

MY SUPPORT TEAM

1. Draw a small circle in the space below. Inside the circle write your name.
2. Make a larger circle around the first one and list the members of your family who support you.
3. Add another circle and list your extended family. This can include uncles and aunts, grandparents, and any other members of your extended family who support you and your endeavors.
4. Add more circles that include friends, teachers, and other people who support you.
5. Decorate your picture of concentric circles with things that have meaning to you.

Keep this picture someplace where it can remind you of all of the people who are part of your support team. As time passes, you will want to redo the list. Refer back to it any time you feel in need of a little more support.

SUCCESS SECRET #101

Lean on each other when things are hard.

Human beings are social creatures. Even if you renew through solitude, you still need people in your life: a support team. The previous success secret gave you a chance

> *"My family makes getting through the stress so much easier."—Nona, age 9*

to discover all of the different members of your support team. It also gave you a chance to remember all of the reasons they are important to you. But, none of that matters if you forget to lean on them when things are hard.

Maybe you were taught that you should stand on your own two feet all of the time. Maybe you think leaning on your friends and family makes you weak. The truth is that we all need someone to turn to from time to time.

Life can be hard, especially when you're gifted. Sometimes your own intensities may get the better of you. Having friends and family to lean on makes the journey a little easier.

Parents Sound Off

Parents know how important a strong family unit can be, and they struggle with how their kids interact with each other. Take a look at the following quotes and talk with your parents about their feelings. You may learn something new.

» "(My child's) sister is one of the few that she lets herself be silly with."—Cho
» "(My kids) have been each other's best friends and partners in crime since childhood. I'm glad they have each other."—Jennifer
» "My daughter is so hard on herself, even when we remind her that she needs to relax. I think it just goes with the territory."—Lien

» "When push comes to shove, my kids know I'll always be their biggest fan. Of course, that doesn't keep them from driving me insane from time to time."—Kristine

Remember, no one really understands you like your family. And although there may be conflict, learning to respect and lean on each other can set you up for lifelong relationships you will treasure.

Being accepted in one's family is something every child has a right to experience. Sadly, however, this doesn't always happen. Read through the tips in this chapter and reflect on the following questions as you look at how you are connected to those most important in your life. And, if you struggle to connect with your family, look for ways to connect with others who can support you as you go from being a child to an adult.

What Do You Think?

Feeling accepted in your family is something every child needs and wants. Take some time to think about the following questions and determine the ways in which you feel connected.

HOW DO YOU KNOW THAT YOU ARE ACCEPTED IN YOUR FAMILY OR WITH YOUR FRIENDS? ARE THERE OTHER ADULTS YOU FEEL CONNECTED TO? WHO ARE THEY?

WHEN YOU DO SOMETHING HURTFUL, HOW DO YOU MAKE AMENDS AND MOVE FORWARD?

IF A FRIEND WASN'T FEELING CONNECT TO HIS FAMILY, WHAT ADVICE WOULD YOU GIVE HIM TO IMPROVE THE SITUATION?

In the End

Facing life as a gifted kid can be a somewhat unique experience. At times it'll be a blast as you get to stretch that beautiful mind of yours, discovering new and sometimes amazing things. Other days you may wish you never were given the label of gifted. You'll be intense, frustrated, and emotional. You may get annoyed with school, your friends, and your parents. It may feel hard being gifted. You may even be tempted to try to not be smart anymore.

However, you know that won't work. Like it or not, you are an amazing gifted kid!

My hope is that you find something in these pages to help you along this journey, something to remind you that you aren't alone as you work through your more intense nature, and something to make the job of growing up a little easier.

The success strategies, although simple, are not always easy to master. You may get frustrated as you attempt them—that's OK. Just go through and attempt that ones that you can. Revisit the book as things come up. What worked today may not work for you tomorrow.

To end things, I wanted to share some final thoughts from parents and kids just like you—their ideas about growing up gifted.

Parents Sound Off

Parents know that growing up is difficult regardless of labels or anything else. Being gifted just adds another layer to the experience—one that has benefits and drawbacks. The following quotes are their ideas about the world of giftedness and their children. Read over their thoughts and then talk with your parents and see what they think about raising a gifted child.

» "I think my relationship with my gifted child comes from an understanding of what it was to be labeled gifted as a child myself and always feeling like I was swimming upstream."—Kathleen

» "The biggest part is to make sure they know they are accepted for who they are and are loved very much for everything they are."—Thomas

» "Being gifted doesn't mean my daughter is good at everything she tries—that is what I want people to realize."—Nichole

» "The hardest, and most important, part of parenting my gifted kid is knowing how to help him stay grounded without quashing his creativity or dreams. It has been a constant balancing act."—Lu

What Do You Think?

Before you reflect on your own final thoughts about growing up gifted, I want you to take a minute and read what some other kids just like you believe.

» "People need to know that being gifted means I'm intense sometimes—with school, with my friends, with everything. I'm not strange or crazy because I'm this way."—Matwa, age 11

» "Being gifted is awesome. Just embrace it. You can't really change it anyways."—Ben, age 9

» "Being in GATE means you have a lot of strengths, but don't forget you still have troubles—things you aren't good at. It's hard to remember that sometimes."—Kimberly, age 10

» "I'm in a gifted class at school. It's cool because people get me, but it's also really hard. Everyone is so smart. Now I feel like I'm left out—like I'm not as smart."—Liam, age 9

» "I wish my teachers understood that being gifted doesn't mean I'm good at everything. Not even close."—Janice, age 12

Most kids recognize that being identified as gifted is a good thing. However, they also know that people make assumptions about gifted kids and sometimes things can be very hard.

Now it's your turn. Take a moment to reflect on everything you have learned through the book and then answer the questions on the next page.

Come back and look at the questions often. As you grow and change, so will your answers. The important thing to remember is that *you* are an amazing person. Embracing your giftedness, both the good parts and the not-so-good parts, will only make you even more amazing.

I would love to hear from you in the future. So drop me a line and tell me how the Success Secrets helped you. Or add your advice to the conversation to help others. Together we can show the world just how fabulous giftedness really is.

**WHICH SUCCESS SECRET
HELPED YOU THE MOST? WHY?**

**WHICH SUCCESS SECRET GAVE
YOU THE MOST TROUBLE? WHY?**

**HOW DO YOU FEEL ABOUT
BEING GIFTED?**

General Information
on Giftedness

Information related to giftedness can sometimes be hard to find. Fortunately there are a few fantastic websites that provide information on every topic imaginable as it relates to giftedness, advocating for the gifted, and the most recent research in the field. Here are a few of my favorite and most-trusted websites:

1. **The National Association for Gifted Children** (http://www.nagc.org): This is a great site for everything from advocacy efforts to the latest research in the field.
2. **Supporting Emotional Needs of the Gifted** (http://www.sengifted.org): This site includes great articles related to the social and emotional needs of gifted children. Also, it's a great source for information related to forming parent support groups.
3. **Davidson Institute for Talent Development** (http://www.davidsongifted.org): This is an excellent site for articles related to giftedness.

4. **Hoagies' Gifted Education** (http://www.hoagiesgifted.org): Hoagies' is a fantastic site for information about giftedness and links for parents and kids to explore.

Books for Gifted Kids

Growing up as a gifted kid can be challenging. For additional tips on dealing with emotional intensity, anxiety, or perfectionism, check out these great books:

1. *Smart Teens' Guide to Living With Intensity; How to Get More Out of Life and Learning* by Lisa Rivero (Great Potential Press, 2010): This is a nice book for teens with additional strategies for living an intense life.

2. *Anxiety-Free Kids: An Interactive Guide for Parents and Children* by Bonnie Zucker (Prufrock Press, 2008): This is a terrific guide for children and parents dealing with anxiety.

3. *When Gifted Kids Don't Have All the Answers: How to Meet Their Social and Emotional Needs* by James R. Delisle and Judy Galbraith (Free Spirit Publishing, 2002): This is good book geared for children and the problems they tend to face in the educational setting.

4. *What to Do When Good Isn't Good Enough: The Real Deal on Perfectionism: A Guide for Kids* by Thomas S. Greenspon (Free Spirit Publishing, 2007): This is good resource for younger children that provides lots of practical strategies.

5. *Calming the Family Storm: Anger Management for Moms, Dads, and All the Kids* by Gary D. McKay and Steven A. Maybell (Impact Publishers, 2004): This is an excellent book full of practical strategies for anger management for all members of the household.

6. *Stick Up for Yourself: Every Kid's Guide to Personal Power and Positive Self-Esteem* by Gershen Kaufman, Lev Raphael, and Pamela Espeland (Free Spirit Publishing, 1999): This is a great resource for kids in learning to deal with most forms of bullying.

Banner, V. (2008). *5 amazing breakthroughs discovered by accident.* Retrieved from http://www.qualityhealth.com/health-lifestyle-articles/5-amazing-breakthroughs-discovered-accident

Cassady, J. C. (2004). The impact of cognitive test anxiety on text comprehension and recall in the absence of external evaluative pressure. *Applied Cognitive Psychology, 18,* 311–325.

Cassady, J. C., & Johnson, R. E. (2002). Cognitive test anxiety and academic performance. *Contemporary Educational Psychology, 27*(2), 270–295.

Coloroso, B. (2009). *The bully, the bullied, and the bystander.* New York, NY: Harper Collins.

HowStuffWorks. (2007). *9 things invented or discovered by accident.* Retrieved from http://science.howstuffworks.com/innovation/9-things-invented-or-discovered-by-accident.htm

National Association for Gifted Children. (2010). *Redefining giftedness for a new century: Shifting the paradigm.* Retrieved from http://www.nagc.org/index.aspx?id=6404

Silverman, L. K. (1989). Invisible gifts, invisible handicaps. *Roeper Review, 12,* 37–42.

Sword, L. (2006a). *Psycho-social needs: Understanding the emotional, intellectual and social uniqueness of growing up gifted.* Retrieved from http://talentdevelop.com/articles/PsychosocNeeds.html

Sword, L. (2006b). *The gifted introvert.* Retrieved from http://talentdevelop.com/articles/GiftIntrov.html

Webb, J. T., Gore, J. L., Amend, E. R., & DeVries, A. R. (2007). *A parent's guide to gifted children.* Scottsdale, AZ: Great Potential Press.

Christine Fonseca has worked in the field of education for more than 10 years. Relying on her expertise as a school psychologist, she has been a resource to parents and educators for understanding the social and emotional needs of gifted children. She holds a master's degree in school psychology and has served as a school psychologist, speaker, consultant, parenting coach, and trainer. Currently, Christine conducts trainings for parents and educators in the Southern California area, where she lives with her husband and gifted daughters. She recently released her other book about gifted kids, *Emotional Intensity in Gifted Students* (Prufrock Press, 2010).

In addition to writing books related to giftedness, Christine writes novels for teens that deal with the often intense emotions felt during adolescence. When she is not directly working with children and parents, she spends her time at her favorite coffee house, writing her next book. If you would like to learn more about Christine, please visit http://www.christinefonseca.com.